The Tyndale New Testament Commentaries

General Editor: PROFESSOR R. V. G. TASKER, M.A., B.D.

THE FIRST EPISTLE GENERAL
OF PETER

THE FIRST EPISTLE GENERAL OF

PETER

A Commentary by

ALAN M. STIBBS, M.A.

Vice-Principal, Oak Hill College, London

and an Introduction by

ANDREW F. WALLS, M.A., B.LITT.

*Lecturer in Theology, Fourah Bay College
(University of Durham), Sierra Leone*

**Inter-Varsity Press,
Leicester, England**

**William B. Eerdmans Publishing Company
Grand Rapids, Michigan**

Inter-Varsity Press
38 De Montfort Street, Leicester LE1 7GP, England
Wm. B. Eerdmans Publishing Company
255 Jefferson S.E., Grand Rapids, MI 49503

First Edition 1959
Reprinted, December 1983

Published and sold only in the USA and Canada by
Wm. B. Eerdmans Publishing Co.

IVP PAPERBACK EDITION 0 85111 866 6
EERDMANS EDITION 0-8028-1416-6

Printed in the United States of America

Inter-Varsity Press is the publishing division of the Universities and Colleges Christian Fellowship (formerly the Inter-Varsity Fellowship), a student movement linking Christian Unions in universities and colleges throughout the British Isles, and a member movement of the International Fellowship of Evangelical Students. For information about local and national activities in Britain write to UCCF, 38 De Montfort Street, Leicester LE1 7GP.

GENERAL PREFACE

ALL who are interested in the teaching and study of the New Testament today cannot fail to be concerned with the lack of commentaries which avoid the extremes of being unduly technical or unhelpfully brief. It is the hope of the editor and publishers that this present series will do something towards the supply of this deficiency. Their aim is to place in the hands of students and serious readers of the New Testament, at a moderate cost, commentaries by a number of scholars who, while they are free to make their own individual contributions, are united in a common desire to promote a truly biblical theology.

The commentaries will be primarily exegetical and only secondarily homiletic, though it is hoped that both student and preacher will find them informative and suggestive. Critical questions will be fully considered in introductory sections, and also, at the author's discretion, in additional notes.

The commentaries are based on the Authorized (King James) Version, partly because this is the version which most Bible readers possess, and partly because it is easier for commentators, working on this foundation, to show why, on textual and linguistic grounds, the later versions are so often to be preferred. No one translation is regarded as infallible, and no single Greek manuscript or group of manuscripts is regarded as always right! Greek words are transliterated to help those unfamiliar with the language, and to save those who do know Greek the trouble of discovering what word is being discussed.

I PETER

There are many signs today of a renewed interest in what the Bible has to say and of a more general desire to understand its meaning as fully and clearly as possible. It is the hope of all those concerned with this series that God will graciously use what they have written to further this end.

R. V. G. TASKER.

CONTENTS

ACKNOWLEDGEMENT

Scripture quotations from the Revised Standard Version of the Bible (copyrighted 1946 and 1952 by the Division of Christian Education, National Council of Churches, U.S.A.) are used by permission.

CHIEF ABBREVIATIONS

AV	English Authorized Version (King James).
RV	English Revised Version, 1881.
RSV	American Revised Standard Version, 1946.
LXX	Septuagint Version.
Beare	F. W. Beare, *The First Epistle of Peter*, Oxford, Blackwell, 1947. Second Edition, with supplement, 1958.
Bigg	C. Bigg, *The Epistles of St. Peter and St. Jude* (The International Critical Commentary), Edinburgh, T. and T. Clark, 1901.
Blenkin	G. W. Blenkin, *The First Epistle General of Peter* (The Cambridge Greek Testament), Cambridge, University Press, 1914.
Brown	John Brown, *Expository Discourses on 1 Peter*, Edinburgh, Oliphants, Third edition, 3 vols., 1886.
Cranfield	C. E. B. Cranfield, *The First Epistle of Peter*, London, S.C.M. Press, 1950.
Cross	F. L. Cross, *1 Peter: a Paschal Liturgy*, London, Mowbrays, 1954.
Cullmann	O. Cullmann, *Peter: Disciple, Apostle, Martyr*, English Translation, London, S.C.M. Press, 1953.
Dibelius	M. Dibelius, *A Fresh Approach to the New Testament and Early Christian Literature*, English Translation, London, Nicholson and Watson, 1936.
EH	Eusebius, *Ecclesiastical History*.
ET	English Translation.
HDB	James Hastings, *A Dictionary of the Bible*, Edinburgh, T. and T. Clark, 5 vols., 1898–1904.
Hort	F. J. A. Hort, *The First Epistle of St. Peter*, London, Macmillan, 1898.

JTS	Journal of Theological Studies.
Leighton	Robert Leighton, Archbishop of Glasgow (died 1684), *A Practical Commentary upon the First Epistle of St. Peter* (many editions).
Masterman	J. H. B. Masterman, *The First Epistle of St. Peter*, London, Macmillan, 1912.
NTS	New Testament Studies.
RB	Revue Biblique.
Selwyn	E. G. Selwyn, *The First Epistle of St. Peter*, London, Macmillan, 1946.
TR	Textus Receptus.
Windisch	H. Windisch, *Die Katholischen Briefe* (Handbuch zum Neuen Testament), 3rd edition, edited by H. Preisker, Tübingen, J. C. B. Mohr, 1951.
Zahn	Th. Zahn, *An Introduction to the New Testament*, English Translation, Edinburgh, T. and T. Clark, 3 vols., 1909.

PREFACE TO THE COMMENTARY

THE First Epistle of Peter has a divinely-inspired message for Christians of every time and place. Certainly its three main themes are all particularly relevant to the present day. When scientific achievement, the welfare state, and dialectical materialism combine to make our century too wordly-minded, 1 Peter recalls us to the heavenly and eternal outlook, and reminds Christians that they are but strangers and pilgrims here. Similarly, when relief from physical disease, and the provision of physical comfort tend to be treated by some as the primary Christian objective, we need the reminder of 1 Peter that holiness matters more, and that all who would follow Christ must, in a selfish and sinful world, be prepared to suffer for righteousness' sake, and to recognize that God uses suffering for the highest good. Also, when moral standards in so-called Christian countries tend seriously to decline, and when genuine young converts to Christ are tempted to spend their enthusiasm more in words than in deeds, we need the challenge of 1 Peter to express our response to Christ and the gospel in transformed behaviour in relation to our fellow-men. So I have found noteworthy satisfaction in studying this Epistle, and I can but hope and pray that this Commentary may be used to stimulate some to find similar help in what God Himself still has to say through this Epistle.

The Commentary itself follows the verse-by-verse pattern of the earlier titles in this series. But for those who wish to study the teaching of the Epistle on the main Christian doctrines of which it treats I have added a section at the end of the book in which the relevant passages are classified and discussed.

I am greatly indebted to others who before me have essayed the task of expounding this Epistle. Without the aid and inspiration of their works my small contribution would never have been attempted. Particularly one might single out the commentaries by E. G. Selwyn, C. Bigg, G. W. Blenkin, C. E. B. Cranfield, J. H. B. Masterman and Robert Leighton, and the Expository Discourses on 1 Peter by John Brown. I am also indebted to Mr. D. H. Wheaton, M.A., B.D., of Oak Hill College for his help in reading the typescript and making many valuable suggestions, and particularly to Mr. A. F. Walls for his ready co-operation in providing the Introduction.

ALAN M. STIBBS.

PREFACE TO THE INTRODUCTION

ACCORDING to the wise man, one of the things for which the earth is disquieted is a servant when he reigneth. Biblical criticism is an ancillary service: it is the menial servant of the exposition of the Word of God. When it is elevated to the throne, misery ensues from the usurper's rule. But servants in a palace have their uses, and are not without their honour, and it is earnestly hoped that the introductory notes which precede the commentary may serve, in a strictly menial capacity, the reverent search for the meaning and application of the text. They do not attempt to give a full survey of the critical questions associated with the Epistle (those who wish to pursue this may be referred to the works mentioned in the footnotes); still less can they claim any original contribution to their solution. They can have no higher aim than to provide a little help in seeing the book in its original setting.

The author of the Introduction is deeply indebted to many whose competence in New Testament studies is vastly greater than his own. In the fine commentary by Dr. Selwyn, lately Dean of Winchester, he has, like the Blessed Damozel, found some knowledge at each pause, or some new thing to know. To Professor F. W. Beare and to Messrs. Blackwell's, the publishers of his commentary on 1 Peter, warm thanks are due for their considerable courtesy in permitting the use of the galley proofs of the corrections and supplement to the second edition, to which a number of references have been incorporated, while still in the press. Though the standpoint of this book is radically different from that of Professor Beare's all must be grateful for his lively and incisive presentation of his case.

To two other writers on 1 Peter, the author's debt, though more indirect, is still greater. To Professor F. L. Cross, his teacher, he owes more than he can say. And it is right to add that from undergraduate days it has been one of his privileges to benefit constantly from the author of this Commentary, who has ever been to him a veritable doctor of the Scriptures and an unmistakable *Servitor Verbi*. It is now his honour to be associated, in however ancillary a capacity, with his work.

A. F. WALLS.

INTRODUCTION

I. DATA WITHIN THE EPISTLE

THE opening verse of the book claims it as the work of the apostle Peter; v. 1 is also most naturally understood as a further allusion, albeit modestly expressed, to the author's apostolic position. To Silvanus, 'a faithful brother', is ascribed some part in writing, or possibly in the delivery of, the letter (v. 12), which is apparently addressed from 'Babylon', where Mark also is (v. 13), to the Christians of Pontus, Galatia, Cappadocia, Asia and Bithynia (i. 1): provinces which covered a large part of the northern and western areas of Asia Minor.

II. I PETER IN THE EARLY CHURCH

It is not always realized how intensely—and how necessarily—the Christians of the early centuries were concerned with questions of authorship and apostolicity. In the matter with which we are immediately concerned, they were confronted, not simply with 1 and 2 Peter, but with a whole mass of writings purporting to emanate from the great apostle. The problems posed were acute,[1] but their scrutiny of these writings was by no means undiscerning or superficial. The historian Eusebius reveals the view taken early in the fourth century, as the great persecutions came to an end and the age of the Church's ecumenical councils dawned.[2] At this time 1 Peter is accepted as beyond dispute. About 2 Peter there is

[1] Cf. G. Quispel and R. M. Grant, 'Note on the Petrine Apocrypha', *Vigiliae Christianae* vi, 1952, pp. 31 ff.

[2] *Ecclesiastical History*, III. 3.1.

hesitation in places: of the Gospel, preaching, Acts and Apocalypse of Peter, grave suspicion.[1]

Nor, if we turn to the literature of an earlier period, do we find any doubts about 1 Peter reflected or implied. Eusebius explicitly says[2] that 'the ancient elders' made free use of it, and echoes of it have been found in Clement of Rome (c. AD 96) and in Ignatius, Barnabas and Hermas, writings emanating from diverse areas and all belonging to the earlier second century. These coincidences are often slight, but it is unlikely, to say the least, that all should be accidental. And there can be no doubt whatever that Polycarp, another early second-century writer, makes frequent use of it.[3] The fact that Polycarp was probably baptized as early as AD 69 is not without significance in this connection.

Possible echoes of 1 Peter have also been detected in the recently discovered *Gospel of Truth* credibly ascribed to the heretic Valentinus before his final breach with the Church. Van Unnik[4] has shown ground for believing that this curious work deliberately reflects the words of books regarded as authoritative by the church in Rome at a time before AD 145.

None of the writers so far mentioned name Peter as their source: but they indicate the regular use of the work and its widespread reception as authoritative. That they would use it as they do had they any strong suspicion of its Petrine attribution being a fiction is incredible; that it was in their time

---

[1] Cf. the remarks of Serapion, Bishop of Antioch, c. AD 190–210, in Eusebius, *EH*, VI. 12.3: 'We . . . receive both Peter and the other apostles as Christ, but the writings which falsely bear their names we reject, as men of experience, knowing that such were not handed down to us.' Serapion was disturbed at the spread of false teaching which claimed support from the 'Gospel of Peter'.

[2] *EH*, III. 3.1. For lists of these testimonies see A. H. Charteris, *Canonicity*, Edinburgh, 1880, pp. 301–311; C. Bigg, *St. Peter and St. Jude*, 1901, pp. 7–15; and *The New Testament in the Apostolic Fathers* edited by a Committee of the Oxford Society for Historical Theology, Oxford, 1905. The Committee were very scrupulous in their assessments, and lean on the side of caution.

[3] As Eusebius himself noted: *EH*, IV. 14.9.

[4] In *The Jung Codex*, edited by F. L. Cross, 1955, pp. 81–129. The text of the *Gospel of Truth*, with translations, has now been provided by M. Malinine, H. C. Puech and G. Quispel, *Evangelium Veritatis*, Zurich, 1956.

circulating anonymously is very unlikely. Indeed, their contemporary, Papias, whose major work was probably written well before AD 140, seems to have used an epistle of Peter's.[1] With Irenaeus, whose celebrated *Against Heresies* was written *c.* AD 180–190, we reach a period from which a larger and more representative selection of writings has survived: and we find that the Petrine authorship of our book is assumed without question by him and by such writers as Clement of Alexandria and Tertullian.[2] Not only so, but contemporary sources show how well established it is in the life of the Church. Its chords reverberate in the pathetic letter of the persecuted Christians of Lyons and Vienne. It shapes the expressions of apologists like Theophilus and the writer to Diognetus. It lies concealed in the sallies of the intellectual heretics whom Clement parries in Alexandria and in the mountebank sectaries whom Irenaeus exposes in the West. Marcion, of course, had not included it in his canon, for he refused all the non-Pauline Epistles; but there is evidence that he knew it.

It is in this setting that we must judge the significance of its absence, without any comment, from the Latin list of canonical books known as the Muratorian Fragment, of which the original dates from about this period. Suspicions have been raised against the text of the Fragment at this and other points, and it is more than possible that a line has accidentally dropped out:[3] though we may freely admit that there is less evidence of the use of 1 Peter by Latin churches than by Greek.[4]

[1] Eusebius, *EH*, III. 39.17. For the relevance of this cf. Th. Zahn, *Introduction to the New Testament*, ET, Edinburgh, 1909, II, pp. 163 f., 185 f., and F. H. Chase, article 'Peter, First Epistle of', in *HDB*, III, p. 780.

[2] But probably not till towards the end of his life: cf. B. F. Westcott, *The Canon of the New Testament*, 6th edn., 1889, pp. 262 f.

[3] Cf. Th. Zahn, *Forschungen zu Geschichte des Neutestamentliche Kanons*, II. 1, Erlangen, 1890, pp. 105–110, 142. Zahn provides a tentative reconstruction of the text. Cf. also Bigg, pp. 14 f.

[4] Cf. Westcott, *op. cit.*, p. 263, n. 3: 'There is not the least evidence to show that its authority was ever disputed, but on the other hand it does not seem to have been much read' (*sc.* in Latin churches). That it was not unknown in these churches is shown by its presence in a large number of Old Latin MSS. The original language of the Muratorian Fragment was, however, probably Greek.

I PETER

We may conclude, therefore, that, leaving aside for the moment any possible use of 1 Peter in other New Testament writings,[1] we find abundant evidence of its influence on the thought and expression of early Christians, much of its wide reception and general recognition as Peter's, and none whatever that it was ever attributed to anyone else. The judgment of Chase still stands: 'The only natural interpretation of the facts is that from the first it was regarded as the work of that apostle.'[2]

And there were men in those days not deficient in critical acumen or theological discrimination, nor insensible of the problems presented by the existence of so many writings claiming Petrine authority.

III. I PETER IN THE MODERN CHURCH

The first significant voice raised against the consensus of the ancients seems to have been that of J. S. Semler, a somewhat erratic pioneer of modern critical method, followed some years later by Cludius,[3] whose argument, based on an interpretation of the relationship between 1 Peter and the Pauline Epistles, was expanded and taken further by others as the nineteenth century proceeded. The arguments which most influenced them were: (i) that the language and diction of 1 Peter do not sort with what we know from other sources about the apostle; (ii) that it lacks the irrefragable stamp of a companion of the Lord, the author being self-effacing to the point of colourlessness; (iii) that it reveals a literary and theological dependence upon the Pauline Epistles intrinsically unlikely in Peter and chronologically impossible within his lifetime, and (iv) that the historical situation implied is that of

[1] We may note in passing that 2 Pet. iii. 1, on any view of the origin of 2 Peter save that of its appearance prior to 1 Peter, may be an early testimony to its existence under Peter's own name.

[2] *Art. cit.*, p. 781.

[3] *Uransichten des Christenthums*, Altona, 1808. I have not seen this work, and am dependent upon J. E. Huther, in the 4th edition of Meyer's Commentary, ET, Edinburgh, 1881, pp. 35 f. Huther gives an interesting, though brief, sketch of early nineteenth-century criticism.

a period later than that of the Neronian persecution, the period to which Peter's death is usually assigned. Twentieth-century scholars have been affected by arguments arising from fields of study more recently developed, notably (v) the correspondence between words and phrases in 1 Peter and the vocabulary of the pagan mysteries: this especially in the wake of Reitzenstein's labours on the mystery religions; and (vi) the formal classification of 1 Peter as a sermon, and probably a baptismal sermon; this especially under the impact of the modern study of literary forms.

The explanations of the book offered by those convinced by these propositions are far from being identical. Among representative books to which some reference must later be made are those of M. Dibelius, H. Windisch (later edited by H. Preisker), R. Perdelwitz, E. J. Goodspeed, and for the most recent, as well as the most forceful, exposition in English, Dr. F. W. Beare.

The patristic confidence in Petrine authorship has, however, never been entirely abandoned. It would not be difficult to quote an impressive list of scholars who have accepted or defended it; nor would all the names be associated with a general conservatism in critical matters. Others have confessed it difficult to decide, and preferred to treat it as an unsolved problem.[1]

Among modern British commentaries two stand out, and both accept the work as Peter's; the noble posthumous fragment by Hort, and the learned and luminous treatment by Dean Selwyn. Sir William Ramsay, in the lectures at Mansfield College which form the basis of his *Church in the Roman Empire*, contended that the references in 1 Peter to persecution presupposed a date *c.* AD 75–79 and thus outside the apostle's lifetime. Conversation with Hort, however, led him to recognize the strength of the arguments that the book might be the

---

[1] E.g. Kirsopp Lake, by no means a conservative critic, clearly finds it hard to discard the unwavering early testimony to the book in favour of the late date he prefers for the persecution passages. Cf. his article 'Peter' in the 11th edn. of *Encyclopaedia Britannica*, and his *Introduction to the New Testament*, 1938, pp. 165 ff.

work of Peter;[1] so much so that, in order to reconcile this with his dating of the persecutions, he suggested an extension of the life of Peter which defied tradition and probability. In this he has had few followers,[2] and 'it seems that the real choice is between accepting the Petrine authorship, thus ascribing the epistle to a date in the time of Nero, or putting it into the days of Trajan and Pliny'.[3]

IV. IS 'PETER' A PSEUDONYM?

Most of those who date the book later than Nero's reign regard it as a pseudepigraph: that is, a work deliberately written under the name of someone other than the true author. Not all who do so hereby attribute unworthy motives to the composer. Dr. Beare, for instance, says, 'The Christians of Asia Minor must have known that Peter was long since dead . . . they would recognize the pseudonym for what it was—an accepted and harmless literary device, employed by a teacher who is more concerned for the Christian content of his message than for the assertion of his own claims to authority'.[4]

Unfortunately, we have no evidence that early second-century Christians would in fact have so received it. On the contrary, it is very hard to imagine the Asian bishops, Polycarp and Papias, mature men at the time many propose for the composition of 1 Peter, living near, possibly even in, the area to which it is addressed, and very conscious, like all their generation, of the great gulf fixed between the original apostles and themselves, recognizing the device as either accepted or harmless. If they did, at what point did their successors cease

---

[1] *The Church in the Roman Empire before AD 170*, 7th edn., 1903, p. 283 n. Cf. also Ramsay's 'Church and Empire in the First Century', *Expositor*, 4th series, vol. VIII, 1893, especially pp. 282–296. In his later work, *Pauline and Other Studies*, 1906, pp. 260 ff. he appears to speak quite confidently of Petrine authorship.

[2] An isolated example is Mr. P. Gardner-Smith, *Encyclopaedia Britannica*, 14th edn., vol. 17, s.v. 'Peter, First Epistle of'. Cf. also H. B. Swete, *The Gospel according to St. Mark*, 1908, p. xxii.

[3] K. and S. Lake, *Introduction to the New Testament*, 1938, p. 167.

[4] F. W. Beare, *The First Epistle of Peter*, Oxford, 1947, p. 29.

to recognize it, and come to take the Petrine attribution at face value? This is not the place to discuss further the implications of pseudepigraphy, or the attitude of ante-Nicene catholic Christians to it,[1] but it is fair to say that the strong attestation of 1 Peter has often been an embarrassment to the theory of pseudepigraphic origin;[2] however severe the cross-examination, 1 Peter always has an alibi. It was always somewhere else at the time.

It is this fact that probably gives rise to alternative theories that the Epistle was originally anonymous: that its attribution to Peter was accidental, the idea, perhaps the surmise, of a later editor who added the opening and closing verses.[3] Such suggestions smack of despair. They require that the book was written well after Peter's death: that in its anonymous state it circulated widely and was much used, and was only *then* given a local habitation and a name (habitation in a number of vigorous churches, the name of a mighty apostle, together with the somewhat inconsequential mention of Mark, Silvanus and 'Babylon'), which were universally and unquestioningly accepted within a relatively short time. The Epistle to the Hebrews may afford an example of an anonymous publication which came to be attributed to an apostle, namely Paul: but no-one ventured to add an apostolic signature to Hebrews, and the great ante-Nicene scholars were under no allusion as to the difficulties of ascertaining its authorship.[4]

What, then, are we to make of the closing words with their

---

[1] But cf. the remarks of D. Guthrie, 'Tertullian and Pseudonymity', *Expository Times*, LXVII, 1956, pp. 341 f.

[2] This appears to have been the judgment of Kirsopp Lake, *art. cit.*, who speaks of the hypothesis of an origin in the time of Pliny as necessitating some such solution as anonymous circulation.

[3] E.g. A. Harnack, *Die Chronologie der altchristlichen Literatur bis Eusebius*, Bd. I, Leipzig, 1897, pp. 451 ff., who holds that Peter's name was attached to the work to guarantee its apostolicity in the days when the Canon was forming. A. C. McGiffert, *A History of Christianity in the Apostolic Age*, Edinburgh, 1897, pp. 593 ff. sees in the attribution to Peter merely an innocent scribal guess. His own guess—it is hardly more—is that the real author was Barnabas.

[4] 'Who wrote the Epistle', says Origen, 'in truth, God knows.' Eusebius, *EH*, VI. 25.14.

reference to Silvanus and Mark? Some have seen in them a covert allusion to the composition of the book by Silvanus, who diffidently hid behind a more illustrious name;[1] but this strains credulity still further, as well as imparting a nasty flavour to the commendation in v. 12. More usual is the view of Beare, who sees the references as having no significance except as part of the apparatus of pseudonymity:[2] and presumably the same thought lies behind the statement of Dibelius that they point to an origin 'in the neighbourhood of Peter'. But this starts new difficulties, for what is there outside this letter to connect Silvanus with Peter or with Rome? Assuming, as is usual, that this Silvanus is the same as the Silas of Acts, we do not hear of him elsewhere in the New Testament later than the middle of Paul's second missionary journey.[3] Mark we hear of as a desirable companion for *Paul* in the sixties,[4] though reliable early tradition does associate him with Peter. As far as our knowledge goes, therefore, it appears that the pseudepigraphic machinery could have been made much more convincing by using, not Silvanus, but, say, Mark as the intermediary, or Clement, the never-failing repository of the pseudo-apostolic tradition of later years.

And so unobtrusive is the machinery, so restrained the references to the apostle, that the contrast with such writings as we can reasonably regard as undoubtedly pseudonymous could hardly be greater. And so difficult is it to imagine a motive for pseudonymity (why should not a letter addressed to a specific situation be sent in the straightforward way that Ignatius and Polycarp sent theirs?) that some critics have

---

[1] E.g. H. von Soden, in Holtzmann's *Hand-Commentar zum Neuen Testament*, Freiburg-im-Breisgau, 1891, pp. 114 ff.; cf. his *History of Early Christian Literature* (ET, 1906), pp. 281 ff. Not dissimilar theories are sometimes urged to associate Tychichus with the composition of Ephesians: see W. L. Knox, *St. Paul and the Church of the Gentiles*, Cambridge, 1939, p. 203 and cf. C. L. Mitton, *The Epistle to the Ephesians*, Oxford, 1950, p. 268.

[2] So the first edition. In the second edition he accepts a Roman origin for the Epistle.

[3] Acts xviii. 5; 2 Cor. i. 19.

[4] 2 Tim. iv. 11.

found in the combination of these facts a strong argument for Petrine authorship.[1]

It seems that in the case before us there is no tenable middle term: either 1 Peter is the work of the apostle whose name it bears, or it is a pseudepigraph. And we have seen that the hypothesis of pseudepigraphic origin is beset with such grave initial difficulties that only overwhelming evidence could render it anything like probable. As we look briefly at other aspects of the writing of the Epistle, we may ask ourselves whether such is the case.

V. LANGUAGE AND DICTION

The Greek of the Epistle is formally good, rhythmic, polished and elegant: it has a certain delicacy absent, for instance, from the torrential eloquence of Paul. There are many quotations from and allusions to the Old Testament, and invariably these follow the Septuagint or Greek version in such a way as to suggest that the author was very familiar with it.

Now the Peter of the Gospels is a Galilean fisherman, who normally speaks Aramaic with an unmistakable north-country accent. He is explicitly described in Acts iv. 13 as 'unlearned and ignorant'. Even allowing for the improvement in Greek which missionary work in Gentile areas—commenced, incidentally, rather late in life—would bring, could he be responsible for such delicate balance of phrase and felicitous choice of words? Could he also have become so intimate with the Septuagint?

'The question', said A. H. McNeile, 'does not admit of a

---

[1] So e.g. J. Moffatt, *Introduction to the Literature of the New Testament*, 3rd edn., Edinburgh, 1918, pp. 334 f. Professor Goodspeed, however, finds a motive in the need to reply to the claim of the Epistle to the Hebrews that the church of Rome should teach the other churches: and to the pouring forth by Revelation, written in the name of an apostle, of hate against the Roman Empire—hence the reference to 'Babylon'. (*Introduction to the New Testament*, Chicago, 1937, pp. 267 ff.) Like so many of the original opinions of this patriarch of scholars, the case is put with such unction and charm that it seems almost boorish to ask for more evidence than he provides.

confident answer.'[1] Dr. Beare is less reticent: 'Such a letter', he says, 'could not have been written by him, the illiterate fisherman, if he had lived to be over a hundred.'[2]

Before we go further, we should note that Peter's ineptitude, both in general education and in Greek in particular, can be exaggerated. In Acts iv. 13, *agrammatos*, translated 'unlearned', does not necessarily mean 'illiterate': in context it probably means 'without formal training in the Scriptures'. The wonder was that these raw laymen could withstand the fathers of Israel so confidently on a point of high theology.[3] Nor need we assume a Galilean to be Greekless, or restricted to fishmarket pidgin. Greek must have been understood and, where necessary, spoken, very widely in Palestine as a second language. Greek personal and place names, Greek coins, Greek loan words meet us everywhere. It was a subject state, in an area where the cosmopolitan language was Greek, and anyone with much to do with public affairs or commerce would need fluency in it.[4] To say then, as Beare does, that 'it is quite probable that there was some bilingualism in Galilee'[5] is a significant understatement. Lieberman has shown that the old idea

[1] *Introduction to the Study of the New Testament*, 2nd edn. revised by C. S. C. Williams, Oxford, 1953, p. 220.

[2] Beare, p. 29.

[3] *Agrammatos* in the papyri often means 'illiterate', but the meaning 'uneducated' can also be supported. The word *idiōtēs* used in Acts iv. 13 generally denotes the 'amateur' or layman in a field (see K. Lake and H. J. Cadbury in *The Beginnings of Christianity*, 1933, IV, p. 44). In the Jewish setting, *gramma* and its cognates have long been associated with the Scriptures. So in Jn. vii. 15, the astonishment is that Jesus knows 'letters' (*grammata*) though He has never learned. The astonishment arises, not from His *writing* anything, but from His teaching in the Temple, teaching learned in no Rabbinic school, but from the source indicated in verse 16.

[4] For a thorough examination of the evidence for the use of Greek in Palestine see Zahn, I, pp. 34–72; and, from a rather different angle, S. Lieberman, *Greek in Jewish Palestine*, New York, 1942. The great grammarian J. H. Moulton supports Zahn's findings, and offers a comparison with bilingual areas in Wales. People from the area would use Greek, their second language, in different qualities according to their education, but 'would write as men who had used the language from boyhood, not as foreigners painfully expressing themselves in an imperfectly-known idiom' (*Grammar of New Testament Greek*, 3rd edn., 1906, I, pp. 6 ff.).

[5] Beare, p. 28.

that Greek was forbidden to strict Jews of the Jerusalem tradition is baseless;[1] what then are we to think of the area which even in Isaiah's time was 'Galilee of the Gentiles', thoroughly interpenetrated by foreigners, with whom the strictest Jews must live and work and trade, and of a man whose own brother Andrew, and fellow-citizen Philip, have wholly Greek names?

Further, many have gone too far in stressing the rhetorical and 'Attic' character of the Greek: Semitic expressions are noticeable as well as classical.[2]

Similarly, we cannot deny to Peter the possibility of early familiarity with the Septuagint. Greek culture and literary methods had invaded even the religious sphere of highly orthodox Jews.[3] Greek-speaking Hellenist Jews formed their own synagogues in Palestine;[4] and Acts shows us the Jerusalem church with a large body of these Hellenist Jews.[5] It also depicts James, the Lord's brother, who must have been as Galilean as Peter himself, delivering a speech in which a Septuagint rendering reinforces a point.[6] And Justin Martyr, born and bred in Samaria in the early years of the second century, uses the Septuagint in all his writings.[7] The Septuagint was, after all, the Authorized Version for the majority of early Christians: can we not expect familiarity with it on the part of all associated for long with the Gentile mission and Greek preaching?

VI. THE SILVANUS HYPOTHESIS

When due weight has been allowed to the preceding consider-

---

[1] S. Lieberman, *Hellenism in Jewish Palestine*, New York, 1950, pp. 100 ff.

[2] One example, the participle used as an imperative, is shown to reflect Semitic use by D. Daube in an appendix to E. G. Selwyn, *The First Epistle of St. Peter*, 1946, pp. 467-488.

[3] Lieberman, *op. cit., passim.*

[4] Cf. G. Dalman, *Jesus-Jeshua*, ET, 1929, p. 3.

[5] This, the usual interpretation of Acts vi, seems preferable to the contention of H. J. Cadbury, *Beginnings of Christianity*, V, pp. 59 ff. that Gentiles are intended.

[6] Acts xv. 14–18. The Epistle of James also regularly uses the Septuagint for its quotations. The connection of either or both with James the Lord's brother may, of course, be denied: but see R. V. G. Tasker, *The General Epistle of James*, in this series, pp. 20 ff.

[7] Cf. Moulton, *op. cit.*, p. 8 n.

ations, many will still feel that the difficulty is not entirely removed. At this point we may return to ponder the exact meaning of v. 12. In what sense is the letter 'by' Silvanus, and who was this 'faithful brother'?

On the first question, several courses are open. Silvanus might be the bearer of the letter; or he might be the secretary to whom it was dictated; or he might have a share, small or large, in its composition. And a combination of functions— both composing and bearing—could be envisaged. Silas in Acts xv. 22 f. is a messenger, and there 'sent by' is used to express this meaning. One would expect some similar construction in v. 12 were Silvanus to be taken as merely the bearer. It is almost certain that this verse accords him a literary function.

The composition and publication of letters and books in the Hellenistic world is a fascinating subject which deserves more comprehensive and comparative study than it has received. The practice of dictation was extremely common. Paul seems to have dictated Romans to Tertius,[1] and certainly later Christian writers used this method.[2] But contemporary literature attests that, with letters particularly, secretaries were often entrusted with very considerable powers. The principal would give the gist of what he wished to say, revise it after the secretary had drawn up the document, perhaps add a few words of his own,[3] and finally seal it. It was his, originating from and guaranteed by him.[4]

---

[1] Rom. xvi. 22.

[2] Examples from papyri and inscriptions are given in G. Milligan, *The New Testament Documents*, 1913, pp. 241 ff. See also the bibliography given by B. M. Metzger, article 'Stenography and Church History' in *Twentieth Century Encyclopaedia of Religious Knowledge*, Grand Rapids, 1955, II, pp. 1060 f. Eusebius (*EH*, VI. 23.2) gives a pleasant picture of the indefatigable Origen keeping fully occupied seven secretaries and as many copyists, supplied by the bounty of a rich friend.

[3] Is 2 Thes. iii. 17–18 an example of this? Gal. vi. 11–18 may be another, though, if so, we must conclude that Galatians was dictated: it could not have been 'written up' by another.

[4] A valuable comparison between classical and Pauline methods is carried out by J. A. Eschlimann, 'La Rédaction des Epîtres Pauliniennes', *RB*, LIII, 1946, pp. 185 ff.

Such may well have been the case with our letter. It would originate from and be guaranteed by Peter, but the expression, the elegant diction, the easy use of the Septuagint—and who can tell how much else?—may be that of Silvanus. It is all but universally agreed that this Silvanus is the missionary of that name mentioned in several of Paul's letters and called Silas in Acts.[1] If this be the case we know a little more about him than is sometimes admitted.[2] He was a Jew, but a Roman citizen; a prophet and a devoted worker in the Gentile mission. His status was such that he was one of the two entrusted with the delicate mission of conveying and explaining the decree of the Jerusalem council to the Gentile Christians. He had worked with Paul, and had been associated with him in the sending of 1 and 2 Thessalonians.[3] The marked use of the first person plural in Thessalonians, together with the occasional irruption of the first person singular, has often been observed: and Paul does not use his personal pronouns loosely.[4] This suggests that Paul is linking his companions with himself more closely than in other letters, and that the changes from 'we' to 'I' have particular significance. This would be particularly the case were one of them responsible in whole or part, for the initial drafting of the letters. If so, was it Silvanus?

Many scholars have attributed a similar function to Silvanus in the composition of 1 Peter, but it is a distinctive feature of Dean Selwyn's commentary to attempt a full demonstration of its intrinsic probability from what we know, or may fairly deduce, about Silvanus. Dr. Beare may be right in indicating that some assumptions made about his personality and abilities go beyond this,[5] but Selwyn's main thrust does not lie here. He draws attention to connections of thought and

[1] Fully argued by P. W. Schmiedel, article 'Silas, Silvanus', *Encyclopaedia Biblica*, IV, cols. 4514–4521. Bishop Lightfoot, however, points out that this falls short of complete proof (*Notes on the Epistles of St. Paul*, 1895, p. 7).

[2] Beare says that we know little more than that he sometimes accompanied Paul and was early associated with the Gentile mission (p. 28).

[3] Acts xv. 22–xvii. 15; 1 Thes. i. 1; 2 Thes. i. 1; 2 Cor. i. 19.

[4] Cf. W. F. Lofthouse, ' "I" and "We" in the Pauline Letters', *Expository Times*, LXIV, 1953, pp. 241 ff.

[5] Beare, 2nd edn., pp. 189 f.

wording between 1 Peter, 1 and 2 Thessalonians, and the Apostolic Decree of Acts xv. The evidence is too extended and complex to be set out here, and must be studied at length in Essay II appended to his commentary.[1] Different readers will doubtless be convinced or not in different degrees, and different parts of the case will also weigh differently: but he seems to have demonstrated a connection between the four both subtle and suggestive. It may help, for instance, in the exegesis of 1 Pet. iii. 7 and 1 Thes. iv. 3–5 to read one in the light of the other, bearing in mind that the same ready scribe may be responsible for the wording of each. But Dr. Selwyn's claim is that beyond the man Silvanus lie patterns of teaching and collections of 'words of the Lord' drawn up under apostolic and prophetic guidance and to which the prophet Silvanus may have contributed. To this we must allude again later.

Dr. Beare holds that in the pseudepigraphic machinery, Silvanus is represented as amanuensis and no more, and writes off the Silvanus hypothesis as a device of desperation.[2] He argues that a man of the standing of Silvanus might have written in his own name to regions where he had worked, or at least have been mentioned in the salutation. This may be true,

---

[1] E. G. Selwyn, *The First Epistle of St. Peter*, 1946, pp. 365–466, and especially pp. 369–384, 439–461.

[2] The commentaries of Selwyn and Beare appeared almost simultaneously, so that neither was able to use the other's work. In his second edition Dr. Beare has been able to devote some pages to the examination of Dean Selwyn's form of the Silvanus hypothesis, which he finds no more convincing than the earlier version. Very justly, he points out that there are great differences in diction between 1 Peter and the stylistically undistinguished Thessalonians and that his view is confirmed by some close students of Thessalonians, notably B. Rigaux, *Les Epîtres aux Thessaloniciens*, Paris, 1956, pp. 105 ff., who will allow Silvanus no significant part in the composition of Paul's letters. The careful judgment of Fr. Rigaux deserves great respect: but one wonders whether he has not excessively pruned Selwyn's evidence in presenting it. It is perhaps significant that he firmly rejects any direct literary dependence of 1 Peter on Thessalonians, which Beare avows, holding that the collections of the Lord's words and the diffusion of Pauline preaching and exhortation sufficiently explain the connections. It is just these elements which Selwyn, who insists that the connections are too constant to be fortuitous and too scattered for literary dependence, seeks to localize in Silvanus. Beare's further argument from a difference in *tone* between Thessalonians and 1 Peter does not seem cogent.

but it begs the question. If Peter, one of the pillar apostles, desired to write, and had the co-operation of Silvanus, the question of the latter writing himself hardly arises. At any rate, on the pseudepigraphic hypothesis, whoever wrote it found no incongruity in the allusion. All our examples of joint signature come from Paul: we cannot assume that the practice was universal. Nor can we be sure that Silvanus had laboured in the particular parts addressed: and if, as is possible, he was messenger as well as draftsman, he would be able to meet the addressees face to face.[1]

What Dr. Beare regards as the fatal objection to Silvanus, and *a fortiori* Peter, sharing authorship, is the teaching of the letter, and especially the meagreness of references to the Spirit. With due regard to the evidence of Paul and Acts, 'it is impossible to believe that any important leader of that early period could have written about the moral life of Christians without paying any attention at all to the transforming power of the Spirit'.[2] This is ever a precarious form of argument, and it is particularly unfortunate in this instance; for, meagre or not, the doctrine of the Holy Spirit in relation to the moral life is present, and at least as much in evidence as in many of Paul's Epistles.[3] Indeed, one of the Epistles in which it is most to the fore is Ephesians, which Dr. Beare does not regard as

---

[1] This is not 'simply fatuous' (Beare, p. 183), if we allow that only parts of Asia and Galatia would be in question (see further pp. 63 f.). After all, Silvanus had done similar 'deputation work' before over a wide area (Acts xv. 23, 27, 32, 33).

[2] Beare, p. 28.

[3] The Spirit's work in the believer is referred to in i. 2 where it is fundamental to the whole succeeding argument, possibly at iv. 6, and at iv. 14 ('through the Spirit' in av at i. 22 is probably not original). In i. 11, the Holy Spirit is spoken of as indwelling the prophets, and in i. 12 in connection with preaching. Such is the case, too, in 1 Thes. i. 5; in 1 Thes. i. 6, iv. 8, the reference is to the Spirit's work in the believer; v. 19 has a special reference. In 2 Thessalonians only ii. 13 relates to the Spirit's work in the believer. In Colossians, which has much to say about moral renovation, there is only the almost casual reference in i. 8. Philippians has three references to the Holy Spirit, of which two are relevant to the question; Philemon none at all. The high prominence of the doctrine in Paul is largely in Romans, Corinthians, Galatians and Ephesians. For an exposition of the doctrine of the Spirit in 1 Peter see further pp. 182 f.

belonging to the early period at all, but as a work of the second Christian generation![1]

The method of writing presupposed by the Silvanus hypothesis is not entirely a thing of the past. Mr. D. M. Paton has drawn an analogy (in quite a different connection) from a younger Church of today. A Chinese Bishop, speaking a Chinese dialect at home but fluent in English, had several secretaries. One, a European, prepared or revised drafts of material to appear in English. Another wrote classical, another 'communist', others different types of modern Chinese, and each would prepare drafts from English originals to be amended by the Bishop. 'In a situation of this sort, linguistic tests for authenticity are clearly useless; for the styles of the secretaries varied widely. Moreover, tests for consistency of thought have to be used with caution, for the Bishop's expression of his views will be affected by which secretarial mind they go through; and circumstances of all sorts may affect, in fact did affect, the choice of secretary. Authenticity was guaranteed by the presence of the seal. In the case under discussion this formal authenticity did actually reflect the origin of the document in the Bishop's mind.'[2]

It is not suggested that this is a picture of the relation of Peter and Silvanus, but it may serve to show that apostolic authenticity may be compatible with a certain freedom of expression on the part of the intermediary. Beyond this we cannot go: it would be futile to seek to delimit exactly the work of Peter and Silvanus and any pre-existing sources. Some pointers we may think we see. Some form of the Silvanus hypothesis is suggested by the very words of the letter, would be in line with contemporary practice, and offers a reasonable solution of what might otherwise be problematical. It does no violence to the text; nothing has shown it intrinsically impossible or even unlikely. It remains a hypothesis; but in our present state of knowledge it at least deserves the primacy in its own field.[3]

[1] Beare, pp. 9 f.
[2] 'Pseudonymity: a Chinese Footnote', *Theology*, LVIII, 1955, pp. 143 f.
[3] It is of little help to say with Lohse, whose criticism of Selwyn is quoted

VII. THE AUTHOR'S PERSONALITY AND PAST HISTORY

The most divergent judgments are given on the author's personality and background; and in the nature of things, objective criteria are few and hard to distinguish in such a case. The most, therefore, that can profitably be done at this point is to state the present position and to indicate possible lines for reverent thought and constructive study.

None will deny that the author of 1 Peter keeps himself well in the background, and makes no parade of the apostolic status he assumes. While this is for some a convincing argument for the Epistle's authenticity, for others it renders it immediately suspect. It must be confessed that it seems a strange principle by which one work is detected as pseudonymous because it has personal allusions and another because it has not.[1]

Dibelius complains that the writing lacks personal quality—there is nothing of what we could justifiably expect from the

by both Rigaux (*op. cit.*, pp. 109 f., n.) and Beare (2nd edn., p. 192) that with secretary-hypotheses one could attempt to prove the authenticity of any letter. It is equally true that with the methods of stylistic criticism often adopted with New Testament documents one could disprove the authenticity of any. Why the burden of proof should always lie with the defence is not clear. If, as Lohse says, secretary-hypotheses merely introduce new unknowns into the question, it is well to remind ourselves that in the study of these venerable writings we are faced with many unknowns, and submit to being rather less certain than we would like to be. If, as W. L. Knox said in his severe review of Selwyn (*Theology*, XLIX, 1946, pp. 342 f.), we are faced with the question 'Who in the early Church could produce this admirable essay in rhythmical prose of the Attic type?', we cannot claim to know enough to say, as he seems to imply, 'No-one'; we cannot know enough to say that Silvanus could not. And at least secretary-hypotheses have in their favour that they are not a palpable invention but were recognized by the ancients. Thus in the fourth century Jerome found the most natural explanation of the obvious differences between 1 and 2 Peter not even in one being written by Peter himself and the other by a secretary, but in Peter's using *different secretaries* for the two letters (*Epistle* XX). Secretary-hypotheses may involve unknowns, and thereby be suspected of introducing a fresh element of nihilism into New Testament study; but in ancient literature secretaries are unknowns who really exist, and have to be allowed for.

[1] 'If a writer declares his identity in the address only of an Epistle, as is the case in 1 Peter, the address is treated as a forged addition. If he hints in an unmistakable way who he is, as is the case in the Gospel of St. John, his words are regarded as so suspicious, and even indecent, that he must be a forger. If he does both, as is the case in 2 Peter, the evidence against him is often treated as irrefutable.' Bigg, p. 232.

leader of the twelve disciples.[1] Others are even more positive. 'It seems incredible that Peter should show such clear dependence upon the Epistles of St. Paul, with whom he never had any close relations, while he makes little use of the language of Jesus, with whom he had been intimately associated during the whole period of his public ministry, and that he should rely wholly on the words of Deutero-Isaiah, not upon his own reminiscences, in holding forth the example of Jesus' demeanour under suffering.'[2] On the other hand, Dean Selwyn can say of this very passage that it recalls many incidents witnessed by Peter himself,[3] and he finds the apostolic testimony stretching throughout the Epistle.

Is there a quiet suggestion of that testimony in the exordium of i. 8? In the very stress on the fact that they who have not seen, one may overhear the tones of one who had.[4] Certainly it requires boldness to determine that the great passage ii. 20 ff. cannot be the work of one present at the events recalled. Selwyn finds verbal links between this passage, with the exhortation which calls it forth, and Mark's account of the Passion: and there is good reason for connecting Mark's Gospel with Peter. But there are deeper affinities than this. 1 Peter sets forth the Christ in terms of the suffering Servant of Isaiah liii, and Mark does the same. 1 Peter sees His death as a ransom: so, too, does the Lord expound the meaning of His sacrifice in the Markan tradition.[5] Prominent in each work is the theme of the vicarious nature of Christ's sufferings. And, as Oscar Cullmann has pointed out, the servant concept dominates the speeches ascribed to Peter in Acts.[6]

---

[1] M. Dibelius, *A Fresh Approach to the New Testament and Early Christian Literature*, 1936, p. 188.
[2] Beare, p. 25.
[3] Selwyn, p. 30.
[4] Cf. Jn. xx. 29.
[5] Cf. Mk. x. 45 with 1 Pet. i. 18. Knox (*loc. cit.*) refers to such 'Markan' sayings being preserved in 1 Peter 'as by accident', while the 'Lukan' Christ, a pattern to be imitated, dominates the author's thought. In view of the fundamental nature of the servant theme in 1 Peter, this statement seems wholly unjustified.
[6] *Peter* (ET, 1953), pp. 67 ff.

Other New Testament writings, of course, are indebted to
Isaiah liii, but it is surely not coincidental that these writings
connected with Peter's name all bear the impress of the
Servant so deeply that, diverse in form as they are, it can be
described as their central thought about Christ.[1]

If these things be true of Mark and Acts, why should it be
counted a thing incredible that in a letter Peter should speak
of the suffering Saviour in the same terms; the terms in which
he had come to understand those sufferings? Could he have
found more expressive words? If he had, could flesh and
blood, after what he had seen, have borne to use them?

For the writer does not 'rely wholly on the words of Deutero-
Isaiah' in the sense of quoting them strictly in his support; to
use Beare's own description, he is 'expressing his own thoughts
in the familiar language of the ancient Scripture'.[2] It is important to remember that Isaiah liii describes both the Servant's conduct and sufferings and the significance of them;
and the same is true of this passage.[3] It is not simply a description of the Passion and an appeal to imitation: it is a statement
of the inner meaning of that Passion and its outcome: the
redemption which only His sufferings could effect, the healing
which is the result of His stripes uniquely. The natural inter-

[1] Cullmann (*loc. cit.*) holds that Peter's Christological thought was
radically influenced by the Servant concept, and that this accords with
what we learn of him elsewhere. At Caesarea Philippi it is he who expressed
such obtuseness on the need for a suffering Messiah and had to be repulsed.
According to 1 Cor. xv he was the first witness of the resurrection, according to Acts the first to preach the facts he had once found so unpalatable. A
backward look to his denial of his Lord would do much to explain the con-
centration on His sufferings and death in his preaching.
It should be noted that Cullmann is not speaking primarily of 1 Peter,
but of Acts; and he says that if 1 Peter were not genuine it would still be a
monument to what Peter's theology and preaching was known to be.

[2] Beare, p. 123.

[3] See especially J. W. L. Hoad, 'Some New Testament References to
Isaiah 53', *Expository Times*, LXVIII, 1957, pp. 254 f. As Hoad says,
'Ethics is being taught against the background of a theology of the person
and work of Christ based on Is. 53'. This is sometimes forgotten by those
who stress the imitative element in the Epistle: the passage begins with
ethics: but it moves into the declaration of sacrificial and vicarious atone-
ment. It begins with the call to imitation: it ends with what is for ever
inimitable.

pretation of v. 1 is that which sees it as a quiet but definite claim to apostleship and to have seen the manifestation of the 'sufferings and the glory'[1]—the latter probably at the transfiguration.[2] To say that the words are 'to be understood mystically'[3] or mean 'one who has engaged himself to the Paschal life'[4] gives them insufficient substance, and quite fails to explain the sudden intrusion of the first person singular. The intention seems plain enough: and yet the author does not stay to dwell on his own past, but moves on to the point he desires to enforce. A list of passages is put forward by Selwyn which one could hardly urge as sure evidence of Peter's authorship, but which, if Peter were in fact the author, would take on a richer meaning.[5] And he notes that the places in which he finds the Petrine testimony occur in and essentially belong to 'passages which are of fundamental importance to the Epistle and constitute its spinal cord'.[6]

A feature of the Epistle is the constant appearance of sayings of the Lord and reminiscences of His teaching.

Collections of the Lord's words must have formed an important part of the tradition and have been in constant use by

---

[1] Essentially an apostle was a *witness* of the resurrection (cf. Acts i. 22; 1 Cor. ix. 1, xv. 8, 9). Here it is the sufferings more than the resurrection of the Messiah which are foremost in the author's mind: but even this is linked in thought with the subsequent glory. While the primary sense of 'witness' in the Bible is 'testimony to', rather than 'observation of', the one sense passes naturally into the other. The apostles were witnesses of Christ's resurrection, Peter was a witness of the sufferings and glory, because they had *seen* the evidence of these events. It is suspiciously like hairsplitting when Beare urges 'they all forsook him and fled' as meaning that Peter was *not* a witness of the sufferings (2nd edn., p. 191). It is also doubtfully consistent with his complaint that the author does not talk like an eyewitness of the sufferings, and hence cannot be Peter.

[2] This may involve 'a somewhat literal acceptance of the Transfiguration' (Beare, 2nd edn., p. 191) but possibly Peter was also rather a literalist on this subject. Assuming the genuineness of 2 Peter, the words of 2 Pet. i. 16–18 indicate the deep impression which the event made on him; assuming that Epistle to be spurious, they are at least evidence that 1 Pet. v. 1 was early interpreted in this way.   [3] Dibelius, p. 188.   [4] Cross, p. 35.

[5] The following may repay study: (a) i. 3 (the living hope), cf. Jn. xxi. 22. (b) i. 7–9, cf. Lk. xxii. 31; Mk. viii. 29. (c) i. 10–12, cf. Lk. xxiv. 25 ff.; Acts xv. 14 ff. (d) iii. 15, cf. the boastings and evasions of Mk. xiv. 29, 71, and the example of Mk. xiv. 62, xv. 2. (e) v. 2 with Jn. xxi. 15 ff.

[6] Selwyn, pp. 31 f.

the early missionaries. We must not assume, therefore, that
verba Christi are a necessary sign of apostolic authorship.
Selwyn believes them to be characteristic of Silvanus. However, Peter must have been one source of the original material;
and it is interesting that it is Epistles under the names of Peter
and James which bear particularly striking marks of the sayings. In 1 Peter they appear woven into the framework of the
discourse; they are not formal quotations.[1]

There are many other coincidences of language and
thought.[2] It would be most unwise to assume that all are signs
of the direct effect on Peter's mind of certain words of the
Lord, or, if this were the case, to build too much upon it, but
one may safely conclude that the author of 1 Peter, far from
making little use of the language of Jesus, was deeply acquain-
ted with the life and teaching of the Master, and to an extent
quite consonant with what one would expect from a companion of the Lord.

Finally, there is a remarkable body of common thought
between 1 Peter and the speeches attributed to Peter in Acts.[3]
We have already seen how fundamental the Servant concept is
to 1 Peter, to Mark and to Acts ii–iii. The Petrine speeches in
Acts share with 1 Peter the same sense of prophetic fulfilment;[4]
the same insistence on the cross as the foreordained action of
God;[5] the same close connection of the resurrection and

[1] One might compare 1 Pet. i. 16 with Mt. v. 48; i. 17 with Mt. xxii. 16;
i. 18 with Mk. x. 45; i. 22 with Jn. xv. 12; ii. 4 with Mt. xxi. 42 ff.; ii. 19
with Lk. vi. 32 and Mt. v. 39; iii. 9 with Mt. v. 39; iii. 14 with Mt. v. 10;
iii. 16 with Mt. v. 44, Lk. vi. 28 where the same Greek word is used; iii. 20
with Mt. xxiv. 37 f.; iv. 11 with Mt. v. 16; iv. 13 with Mt. v. 10 ff.; iv. 18
with Mt. xxiv. 22; v. 3 with Mt. xx. 25; v. 7 with Mt. vi. 25 ff. These may
not all, of course, be conscious reminiscences.
[2] See the list compiled by E. H. Plumptre, *St. Peter and St. Jude* in the
Cambridge Bible, 1879, pp. 65 ff. Selwyn (pp. 442–449) essays a study of
'Verba Christi' in Acts and the Epistles which he regards as components of
a 'persecution document'. It should be noted, however, that the 'Verba
Christi' are by no means confined to the persecution passages.
[3] For the evidence for accepting these as reflecting substantially what
Peter said, see F. F. Bruce, *The Speeches in Acts*, 1944, and *The Acts of the
Apostles* (Greek Text), 1951, pp. 18 ff. On the relation of 1 Peter to the
Petrine speeches see Selwyn, pp. 33–36; and cf. Zahn, II, pp. 173 f., 186 n. 2.
[4] Acts ii. 16 ff., iii. 18; 1 Pet. i. 10 ff., 20.   [5] Acts ii. 23; 1 Pet. i. 20.

I PETER

exaltation;[1] the same call to repentance and faith-baptism;[2] the same sense of the certainty of Christ's judgment of living and dead.[3] As we compare the apostle who strides through the early chapters of Acts with what we find written in his name, there is again substantial agreement. In both we have a joyous recognition of the Gentile mission and the blessings attending it; expressed, none the less, essentially from a Jewish standpoint.[4] In both we have the conviction of an eyewitness inviting belief.[5] In both, too, we are in an atmosphere where the *Name* of Jesus means much in Christian speech.[6]

There are points of detail which may not be insignificant; the use of the oracle about the stone[7] and the use of *xylon*, properly meaning 'wood', for the cross.[8]

It was said at the outset that in determining the author's personality and antecedents, objective tests would be hard to come by. But at least there seems a body of evidence too considerable for anyone to say lightly that the author was a mere Pauline cipher who could not have companied with Jesus. Moreover this evidence, taken together, makes sense: it binds together the witness of Mark, Acts and 1 Peter: it fits into the general picture of Peter in the New Testament: at the very least it invests the Petrine authorship of the last-named with a certain suitability. Through it all runs like a silver thread the theme of 'the sufferings and the glory'; from the time when Peter recoiled from the idea near Caesarea Philippi as inconceivably repulsive to the time when he called on his brethren to rejoice at their share in Christ's sufferings, that they might rejoice at His manifested glory.[9]

[1] Acts ii. 32 ff.; 1 Pet. i. 21, iii. 22.
[2] Acts ii. 38, 40; 1 Pet. iii. 20 ff.
[3] Acts x. 42; 1 Pet. iv. 5.
[4] Acts x. 9 ff., xi. 17, xv. 7 ff.; 1 Pet. i. 1, 4–12, ii. 3–10.
[5] Acts ii. 32, iii. 15, v. 32, x. 39 f.; 1 Pet. i. 3, i. 8, v. 1.
[6] Acts ii. 21, ii. 38, iii. 6, 16, iv. 12 and many others; 1 Pet. iv. 14 ff. and the title *Christians* (Acts xi. 26; 1 Pet. iv. 16).
[7] Acts iv. 9 ff.; 1 Pet. ii. 7.
[8] Acts v. 30, x. 39; 1 Pet. ii. 24.
[9] Cf. G. B. Stevens, *The Theology of the New Testament*, 2nd edn., Edinburgh, 1906, pp. 294 f.

VIII. THE AUTHOR'S RELIGIOUS BACKGROUND

If what we have so far concluded is valid, the minds and hands behind 1 Peter belonged to Palestinian Jews of the first Christian generation who had had long and fruitful association with Gentiles. Since, however, some have found positive traces of a Gentile and pagan background, it may be well to notice this briefly.

The most considerable essay on this theme is that of R. Perdelwitz,[1] written in days when some scholars were making the most extravagant claims for the dependence of Christianity on the mystery religions. Perdelwitz, however, was not concerned to trace the substance of the Epistle to the mysteries, but he held that its form had been strongly influenced by them; so much so that he judges that both the writer and the recipients were former devotees of a mystery-cult, probably associated with the Phrygian Magna Mater or Cybele. The author presents Christianity as a new and more excellent mystery and baptism as the initiation; the frequent negatives and privative particles (e.g. *in*corruptible and *un*defiled in i. 4) are indications of the superiority of the Christian's blessings; and to the influences of the mysteries Perdelwitz ascribes those concepts for which he can find no parallel in the Hebraic or primitive Christian tradition. These are particularly associated with the 'rebirth', spoken of in i. 3 ff. and i. 23, which in the Cybele and Mithras cults was effected by the *taurobolium* or bath in bull's blood (to which he finds allusion in i. 2 ff., including the 'sprinkling of the blood'), and the teaching on the new spiritual family and priesthood into which the readers have come. He concludes from such knowledge of the history of the cults as is available that the use of this imagery in the area to which 1 Peter belongs demands a date for the letter early in the second century.

Beare, while rejecting the allusion to the *taurobolium*, follows Perdelwitz to the extent of allowing that the contacts with

---

[1] *Die Mysterienreligion und das Problem des 1 Petrusbriefes*, Giessen, 1911. The leading examples he adduces are searchingly examined by Selwyn, pp. 305–311.

the mysteries suggest that the author's past lies in them: and he finds this opinion reinforced by the lack of any concern with Paul's great theme of the place of the Law in the life of God's people, such as one might expect from a Christian Jew.[1] Professor F. L. Cross, in an important recent monograph,[2] holds that the Epistle demonstrates a word-play found elsewhere in early Christian literature, on *Pascha*, 'Easter' and *paschein*, to suffer: and since one word has a Semitic, and the other a Greek origin, it has been suggested that this word-play could have been employed only by a person of Greek background.[3]

Most of this, however, is the most precarious inference. Knowledge of the history of the cults is extremely limited, and even if the contacts were established, it would be foolhardy to use this as if it were solid evidence for the date of the book. But it may be safely said that they have not been established. Perdelwitz has had little following in his theory of an allusion to the *taurobolium*[4] (and how much richer the meaning when the section is expounded with the Old Testament significance of sprinkling in mind!),[5] and many of his other examples are equally slight, or equally explicable from other sources. It might be just as easy to show by the same methods that the author had been a Palestinian Rabbi or a Qumran sectary.[6] It is conceivable that Peter might reinforce a point by reference

[1] Beare, pp. 16 ff., 27. 'If this man was a Jew, he had emancipated himself from his own religious inheritance to a degree that was never possible to Paul.'

[2] *1 Peter: A Paschal Liturgy*, 1954.

[3] It must be said that Dr. Cross himself insists that the authorship of 1 Peter is beyond the scope of his essay; and all the hints that he throws out in his last chapter imply an origin for the book at least in apostolic times.

[4] There is no evidence of this ghastly ritual in the Cybele cult until the middle of the second century. The great Mithraic scholar Franz Cumont held, however, that it had probably been practised in Asia since time immemorial: *The Mysteries of Mithra*, ET, New York, 1956, p. 180.

[5] See the commentary on i. 2. Beare expounds this verse without reference to the *taurobolium* (pp. 51 f.).

[6] It is interesting that some of the references used by Perdelwitz are among those for which Dr. David Daube, in his *The New Testament and Rabbinic Judaism*, 1956, finds Jewish parallels.

to some cult custom known to his readers, but that the contacts are many or significant has not been shown.

It is perhaps worth noting that present attention is focused more usually on the Jewish affinities of the exhortations in I Peter than on the pagan.[1] And one can certainly visualize the man who joyfully saw God's acceptance of the Gentiles into His Israel in the house of Cornelius, and had the lesson sorely reinforced by Paul's rough tongue at Antioch, addressing Gentile Christians as 'the elect sojourners of the dispersion',[2] as he described their state in terms recalling the covenants with the fathers. The standpoint is Jewish: the outlook Christian. How readily, too, might a Christian Jew refer to loose and lawless living as 'what the Gentiles like to do'.[3] Nor does the absence of concern with the place of the Law weigh against this. If we had only the Thessalonian and Corinthian Epistles of Paul we might not guess that he was much concerned with it. As to the suggested word-play on *paschein*, this again is open to question;[4] but even if it were proved, it would be rash to identify the author's background thereby; assonance is commonly employed by preachers without any thought of providing scientific etymologies.[5]

IX. THE THEOLOGICAL AFFINITIES OF THE EPISTLE

Whatever view is taken as to the Hellenistic or Hebraic background of the author all students of the Epistle agree that his theology is thoroughly Pauline. Not only so, but his forms of theological expression are much closer to Paul's than are, say, those of John or James.[6] And this fact remains whether or not we postulate a literary dependence upon Paul.

[1] E.g. Daube, *op. cit.*; P. Carrington, *The Primitive Christian Catechism*, Cambridge, 1940.
[2] See i. 1, RV, and commentary *in loc.*   [3] iv. 3, RSV.   [4] See p. 61 below.
[5] One can think of such preachers' illustrations as the explanation of 'justified' as 'just as if I'd never sinned'.
[6] This is not, of course, to say that there is not an underlying theological unity throughout the New Testament. The essential harmony of Paul, John and James is deep and indeed fundamental, but for some of their great themes they use different vocabularies.

But it can be stated in different ways. The fact that ii. 4 ff. shows a doctrine of the Church in Pauline terms, and a Church where there is no difficulty whatever about the admission of Gentile converts, leads one distinguished scholar to break out: 'If Peter wrote this passage then in his old age he must have become a disciple of Paul's. We have no right to say this of him and thereby rob his figure of a good deal of its independent significance.'[1] Beare rightly insists that 1 Peter is no mere echo of Paul, but is sure that it is the work of a man who has formed himself on the Pauline writings and on a considerable body of them.

To the literary aspect we must briefly allude later. But in strictly theological matters we must ask ourselves what we have a right to expect, what 'independent significance' we wish to give to Peter. The once common idea that Peter and Paul were in constant and necessary opposition is now happily banished to the frontiers of criticism; but its ghost still walks across the centre, and the sharp disagreement to which Paul alludes in Galatians ii is alleged to show that Peter was, at least for a time, out of sympathy with his clear-sighted colleague.[2] But there is not a hint in the passage that Peter's theology was at fault any more than that of Barnabas was; quite the reverse, for his offence in Paul's eyes was the incompatibility of his practice with his theory. He had betrayed the principle of Gentile liberty which he had previously warmly supported, not by word, but by action. His withdrawal from table-fellowship was dictated, not by theological conviction, but by fear of his more prickly Jewish brethren.[3]

In the New Testament we see Peter principally as the apostle of the circumcision,[4] though with an important part to play in the origin of the Gentile mission. Good tradition unanimously declares that his later work extended well outside

---

[1] Dibelius, p. 188. But have we any evidence that over most, or all, of the area addressed there was ever a 'Jewish problem'? Note how the quotation from Hosea ii is modified. These people had not, like old Israel, held a status and lost it: before their conversion they never had been a people. Cf. Zahn, II, p. 143.
[2] E.g. Beare, pp. 26, 30.   [3] Gal. ii. 11 ff.   [4] Gal. ii. 8.

Palestine, and there seems no reason to reject the early accounts, supported by the excellent testimony of 1 Clement, that Peter and Paul both worked in Rome till Nero's persecution cut them off.[1] We have not the slightest reason to believe that Peter's theological convictions differed from Paul's: and in the circumstances to find some of Paul's modes of expression, especially in addressing a Gentile community, is hardly surprising. Nor is another fact that is sometimes overlooked: that there are also links of thought and language with the Epistle of James. It would be readily understandable if Peter should be indebted to each of the two great men with whom he had laboured. The outline 'kerygma' or preaching they all had in common. The apostolic testimony to the words and works of Jesus could be given by Peter almost as by no-one else. And burnt into his consciousness was the figure of the Lord, whom he beheld following His own teaching as the suffering Servant of Jehovah. But for the task of the developed literary expression of these things as the Christian mission proceeded, God had pre-eminently prepared other minds and tongues.[2]

Finally, we must remember that Silvanus had served for many years with Paul.

On such a matter as the attempt to date the theology of the book we are on such notoriously difficult ground, and subjective considerations play so considerable a part, that discussion in small space is hardly profitable. Scholars who favour a late date on other grounds tend to say that it is post-apostolic:[3] others that it is essentially primitive. Two judgments may therefore be quoted because they come from scholars who do

---

[1] Cf. the thorough statement of evidence in Cullmann, pp. 70–152.

[2] Cf. Zahn, II, p. 176. 'From all that we know of Peter there is not the slightest reason to assume that he was original, in the sense that James or Paul or John was original. On the contrary, his nature was such as to make him susceptible to influences from without; while the fact that he recovered so quickly from the errors into which this tendency led him, proves that in doing that which was good and wholesome he did not have to contend with a strongly biassed character.'

[3] So Beare, p. 30. The main specific instance he quotes is the doctrine of the Holy Spirit: but on this see above, pp. 29 f.

not, in the writings where the judgments are made, finally commit themselves on the authorship and date of the book. Kirsopp Lake said, 'The simplicity of the theology is marked, and affords an argument for an early date.'[1] And Dr. Cross says 'the theology of 1 Peter betrays many signs of great antiquity', and goes on to comment on 'that remarkable co-presence of the end as future and yet as already here',[2] from which second-century writings depart.

Dr. Cross poses a final question. 'Does it breathe the spirit of the other biblical writings which we use day by day in our Christian worship, or is it that of later days whose ethos, however sublime, is not that of the New Testament?'

He adds, 'I think that many will have a ready answer.'[3]

X. THE LITERARY AFFINITIES OF THE EPISTLE

In reading 1 Peter one is constantly reminded of other parts of the New Testament. Echoes of certain books in particular keep recurring: Romans, Ephesians, Hebrews and James. Some of the resemblances are so singular as to make it most unlikely that they should be accidental. For instance, as we have seen, 1 Peter uses the Septuagint translation for Old Testament quotations; yet in the passage ii. 4–8 the quotations diverge from the Septuagint: and we find the same divergence in the same quotations in Rom. ix. 32 ff.[4]

If such resemblances as these are not fortuitous, then there are three possibilities: that 1 Peter draws from the other writings; that they draw from 1 Peter; or that both 1 Peter and the others draw from common sources.

The second possibility may be discounted. It has sometimes been urged that Ephesians depends on 1 Peter, but few would undertake to show that all these books do so. The first has frequently been urged; and the author of 1 Peter has been credited with a knowledge of the entire Pauline collection of

[1] *Encyclopaedia Britannica*, 11th edn., vol. XXI, p. 296.
[2] Cross, p. 43.
[3] *op. cit.*, p. 44.
[4] Cf. Selwyn, pp. 268 ff., where this passage is treated at length.

letters.[1] In particular Dr. C. L. Mitton has claimed that 1
Peter draws unmistakably from Ephesians, as Ephesians does
from Colossians.[2] The particular significance of this is that Dr.
Mitton holds that Ephesians originated about AD 90 and therefore 1 Peter must, on this view, belong to the early years of the
second century.[3]

The third way has been espoused with the greatest diligence
and learning by Dean Selwyn, who finds behind all the documents traces of the common pattern of teaching in apostolic
times, and sees their very agreements as evidence of this.[4]

Again we reach a subject so vast and complex that the
merest sketch must suffice here.[5] Not only are the actual facts
of literary dependence in grave dispute, but when a fact is
thought to be established, its significance is variously determined by factors which lie outside our scope. The minute comparison of texts which this study demands involves immense
labour, and one marvels at the unflagging patience of those
scholars who have devoted themselves to it: but it is difficult
to avoid the impression that this type of criticism has distinct
limitations. There is a certain rigidity about it, which together
with the opposing results often obtained, makes one suspect its
universal accuracy in predicting the workings of a vigorous and
well-stored mind, which had treasures to draw on that we

---

[1] E.g. Beare (2nd edn., p. 195) holds that 1 Peter shows knowledge of
several, if not all, of Paul's letters, and several other New Testament
writings, and that he must have had access to the complete Pauline corpus.
On the theory to which Dr. Beare appears to subscribe, the corpus was not
collected until after AD 90. See C. L. Mitton, *The Formation of the Pauline
Corpus of Letters*, 1955, and the review by T. W. Manson, *JTS* (New
Series), VII, 1956, pp. 286 ff., which sharply criticizes the theory.

[2] *The Epistle to the Ephesians*, Oxford, 1951, pp. 176–197, and especially
'The Relationship between 1 Peter and Ephesians', *JTS* (New Series), I,
1950, pp. 67 ff. His general thesis is that where Ephesians, Colossians and
1 Peter have common material, 1 Peter is always closer to Ephesians than
to Colossians.

[3] Cf. Beare, 2nd edn., pp. 195 f., 'as the Deutero-Pauline character of
Ephesians has been amply demonstrated . . . the demonstration of its use by
1 Peter at the same time rules out all possibility of Petrine authorship'.

[4] In Essay II of his commentary, pp. 363–466.

[5] See also, besides the works quoted, the useful summary of recent literature in Beare, 2nd edn., pp. 192 ff.

know not of, and situations to face that we can recognize only in dim outline. For the investigation of a 'scissors-and-paste' document, where diverse written sources have been pieced together (such as one assumes Tatian's Diatesseron, or Gospel Harmony, to have been), it may be a most accurate instrument; but we have no reason to believe that many ancient documents were composed in that way.[1]

The question of the authenticity of Ephesians lies outside our scope; but we may note, first, that neither Dr. Mitton's methods nor his conclusions have carried complete conviction everywhere;[2] second, that we must not use the literary dependence of 1 Peter upon Ephesians, if we hold it proven, as *both* a major pillar of a case for the late date for Ephesians and at the same time for the late date of 1 Peter. This would be arguing in a circle. At least we should be prepared for the argument to be reversed; for if the grounds for holding 1 Peter to be early are good, then it should bring Ephesians with it.[3]

Again we must ask ourselves what we have a right to expect. There seems no *a priori* reason why there should not be a liter-

---

[1] Beare reminds us that 'the use of the techniques of form-criticism does not obliterate the facts of *literary* dependence' (2nd edn., p. 196). But in the Epistles, it is the facts which are so hard to establish. From Mitton's gigantic labours one would imagine the question settled of the priority of Colossians over Ephesians; yet it makes a great deal of difference whether one sees Ephesians as due to a later writer who knows Colossians as a literary work, or to Paul who has just written it: and one remembers the equally gigantic labours of Ernst Percy, *Die Probleme der Kolosser und Epheserbriefe*, Lund, 1946, which conclude for the Pauline authorship of Ephesians. There are signs, too, that the question of the priority of Colossians may be re-opened (cf. J. Coutts, 'Ephesians 1. 3–14 and 1 Peter 1. 3–12', *NTS*, iii, 1957, pp. 115 ff.); and again one is reminded of the nineteenth-century hypothesis of Holtzmann by which, postulating various editions, he sought to explain that sometimes Ephesians and sometimes Colossians was prior—cumbersome and quite impossible (cf., however, C. Masson, *Colossiens*, Paris, 1950), but a witness to a state of affairs most defeating to the purely literary critic, but conceivable if one man's mind lay behind both documents.

[2] See e.g. J. N. Sanders in *Studies in Ephesians*, ed. F. L. Cross, 1955; and, most recently, E. K. Simpson and F. F. Bruce, *Ephesians and Colossians*, 1958.

[3] As Dr. Mitton candidly allows: 'It is true, of course, that if 1 Peter could be confidently ascribed to Peter's lifetime, the fact of the priority of Ephesians would be an almost conclusive argument for its Pauline authorship' (*Epistle to the Ephesians*, p. 196).

ary dependence of Peter on Ephesians, assuming the Pauline authorship of that letter. Indeed, if Peter was at Rome in the days of Nero when these words were written, the letters of Paul to which he would have readiest access might well have been Romans and the 'circular' Ephesians—those letters of which we find the most considerable traces in the Epistle.[1] And we might expect Silvanus, the erstwhile companion of Paul, to have considerable acquaintance with his teaching and letters. But we might also expect that in the apostolic Church there would be patterns of common teaching, and that these would be reflected in writings by different authors.

XI. THE PATTERNS OF CHRISTIAN TEACHING

In the Epistles, we find occasional indications of the materials which the early missionaries employed in their work. Foremost among these are collections of 'words of the Lord' to which Paul refers to answer his Corinthian enquirers.[2] There are also hints of the type of instruction which early converts received.[3] As the gospel spread, and more and more converts came from entirely pagan and perhaps vicious backgrounds,[4] the need for systematic ethical instruction would become increasingly prominent. One would expect such codes of 'paranesis', as they are called, to be associated with, though not restricted to, preparation for baptism: and that in these and other materials used in the world mission in the first century there would be a measure of common tradition. The apostles, who had been appointed by the Lord Himself, still lived, and were the acknowledged guides of the Church.

In this task, moreover, they were following Jewish precedent: converts to Judaism had from time immemorial received similar instruction.[5] In later years we find a considerable time

[1] Cf. Zahn, II, p. 177, who suggests that there were several copies of Ephesians preserved, and available in Rome in AD 64.

[2] Cf. 1 Cor. vii. 10, 12, 25; cf. 1 Thes. iv. 15.

[3] Cf. 1 Thes. ii. 3, iv. 1 ff.; 2 Thes. ii. 5, 15.

[4] Some insight into the past of ordinary members of a Gentile church is given by Paul in 1 Cor. vi. 9–11. Cf. 1 Pet. i. 18, ii. 1.

[5] Cf. D. Daube, *op. cit.*, for examples. Note, too, the thorough instructions in the Community 'Rule' given to novices by the Qumran sect.

—in some instances as long as three years[1]—fixed as the period of 'catechetical' instruction before baptism was permitted.

It is the claim of the Archbishop of Quebec, Dr. Philip Carrington, in a fascinating book[2] to have discerned marks of this common pattern in the New Testament, and he suggests that the pattern explains certain parallels between New Testament documents that would otherwise be attributed to direct borrowing. An example may serve to show the sort of parallel which he believes may be due to the 'catechetical' pattern:

I PETER i. 6, 7	ROMANS v. 3, 4	JAMES i. 2, 3
Ye rejoice	We boast	Count it all joy
Though grieved for a little	In our afflictions	When you fall into
	Knowing that	various temptations
Through various temptations	'Affliction worketh patience	Knowing that 'The testing of your faith
That the testing of your faith	And patience testing	works patience. . . .'
Might be found unto praise. . . .	And testing. . . .'	

If the resemblances are accidental, the coincidences are remarkable: if there is literary dependence, the borrowing has been of a most complex type. But if Peter, Paul and James were all weaving their thoughts round a common apostolic pattern of exhortation for believers, then both the resemblances and the differences are explained.

Carrington believes that from Ephesians, Colossians, James and I Peter, with cross-reference to other Epistles, he can reconstruct the outline of the fourfold general baptismal catechism. We may glance at this as it relates to I Peter.

a. The first section called for the lusts and sins characteristic of the former pagan life (and particularly sins of speech) to be put off as things of the past (I Pet. ii. 1, 11).

---

[1] So Hippolytus, *Ap. Trad.*, xvii. 1 (ed. G. Dix, 1937), about AD 215. Hippolytus had purist tendencies, so this may be on the high side for the period.

[2] *The Primitive Christian Catechism*, Cambridge, 1940. The example quoted is discussed pp. 23 ff.

b. There followed the call to Christian humility, subjection, and subordination of self-interest. Attention is given to the position of particular classes, wives, husbands, slaves;[1] but obligations are involved on all—subjection to the civil power, and subordination of Christians to each other (1 Pet. ii. 12–iii. 9—the passage includes parentheses).

c. Then came the call to watch and pray: regularly occurring in the final exhortation of an Epistle, and found in each of 1 Peter's 'closing' exhortations (1 Pet. iv. 7, v. 8).

d. Finally the command to resist or stand firm against the devil (1 Pet. v. 8, 9).

These considerations shed light on a number of issues. For one thing, some of the closest resemblances between 1 Peter and some other Epistles occur in just these sections, and lead to the suspicion that this, and not direct dependence, was their origin. Again, Carrington points to the interesting fact that much of the teaching on persecution in 1 Peter is held in common with other Epistles, and sees it as part of a common stock of catechetical material. Selwyn, in a careful study,[2] prefers to see a separate body of persecution teaching: a necessary part of early Christian instruction: teaching which saw persecution as a ground of rejoicing, a test of character, a necessary visitation, and a sign of the imminence of divine judgment and vindication, and which was anchored in words of the Lord on the subject.

The 'persecution documents' he finds reflected in 1 Peter and in other Epistles, more particularly 1 and 2 Thessalonians, in which Silvanus again plays a part. He also believes that he can define, more precisely than Carrington attempted, the precise sources used for the general catechism: even to isolating two separate baptismal forms and a separate table of cate- chumen virtues; and he associates Silvanus with the construc- tion of these patterns. He points also to liturgical fragments such as hymns. Whether Dean Selwyn's painstaking analysis

---

[1] In all the other writings, masters are also included; for some reason they are omitted in 1 Peter.
[2] Selwyn, pp. 439 ff. Cf. Beare, 2nd edn., pp. 193 f.

will bear the weight of this enormous structure remains to be seen.[1] Some parts carry more conviction than others. We may, however, be grateful to the Archbishop and the Dean for one of the most constructive movements in modern literary criticism, and one which deserves much more study. It may be asked why, if common forms were recognized, did the apostles write at all?[2] But the suggestion is not that the writers produce the form as it stands; Carrington declares that the complete baptismal form is in any case unrecoverable: obviously they modify, fill out, weave new thoughts in and round it. It is only comparison that brings the form to the surface.

In conclusion we may be allowed two further questions or cautions.

First, may we not too readily associate the form with baptism, perhaps misled by our reading of Jewish practice, and the demands of the later catechumenate? After all, certain of our early sources suggest that the early Christians, rather as in the early Methodist class meetings, solemnly undertook strict moral obligations or received regular moral exhortation during their regular services.[3] This would explain why the form should recur in writings which give us no particular indication that they are intended for catechumens or newly-baptized Christians.

Second, how far are we justified in postulating that all the common tradition we find reflects written documents? Even in our own day some forms of evangelistic and pastoral literature sometimes tend to be stereotyped: similar texts, similar illustrations may be used, without any obvious literary dependence. Two tract writers may reflect a common pattern, and reproduce it so that it can be recognized in its different expressions. But though the pattern is a very real entity, it has never been in written form itself.

---

[1] Cf. the criticism of B. Rigaux already cited. But see above p. 28.

[2] Cf. Beare, 2nd edn., p. 194.

[3] In Pliny's *Letter* xcvi he mentions to Trajan that the Christians took oaths against certain sins. Justin, *Apology*, lxvii, mentions moral exhortation in the Sunday service.

XII. THE PERSECUTIONS IN I PETER

a. *The references to persecution*

Persecution is alluded to four times in the Epistle.

1. In i. 6–7 the readers are rejoicing in the possession of a life governed by the hope of the Lord's manifestation, despite the different trials which they undergo. These will be of short duration; like a goldsmith's furnace, their object is to refine so that their faith may be a choice article when that consummation occurs. A little later (i. 11) reference is made to the sufferings of Christ and the ensuing glory, predicted by the prophets.

2. In iii. 13–17, following upon an exhortation to love and humility, it is suggested that, as a general principle, no-one will harm a Christian for his zeal for righteousness. However, it may happen: Christians may have to suffer 'for righteousness' sake'. Should this be the case, as the Lord's beatitude said, they are happily placed. They need not fear. But let each be sure of the Lordship of Christ in his own heart, be ready to meet all enquiry about the faith, maintaining a humble and reverent spirit while doing so. This will do much to disarm opposition and shame scandalmongers into silence. It is better to suffer for doing right, should such be God's will, than for doing wrong. This again is enforced by the example of Christ's sufferings,—for His were entirely undeserved,—and by the manner in which He bore them.

3. In iv. 12–19, after a doxology which might well have been expected to herald the close of the book, a new exhortation appears. The readers are not to be surprised at the imminent 'fiery trial' (*purōsis*) which was now to be their lot. It is coming to test and refine them. Their position is one for rejoicing: in measure they are sharing such sufferings as Christ received, and may expect to share His glory when it comes. It is a happy thing to be reproached because one is associated with Christ's name: only let them take care that it is for Christ's name, and not for any other cause. A man should glorify God in the name of Christian. Judgment is beginning:

it is about to sift the Church. If God's people undergo such rigorous treatment, what hope is there for His opponents?

4. In v. 9, a call to resist the devil characteristic of the catechetical form, the persecutions are regarded as a principal weapon of his. The readers are encouraged by the remembrance that the same kind of suffering is taking its course in the experience of many Christians in the world at large.

b. *Is the persecution of the same kind in each case?*

In the first two passages, trials exist, unjust suffering is a possibility: in the second two a fierce ordeal is imminent. From iv. 12 onwards the language is more specific. Accordingly, some have urged that iv. 12 ff. comes from a later period than the rest of the letter, and that it reflects a different, and severer, type of persecution. Two letters, or a sermon and a letter, from the same author,[1] have been joined together. If the first envisaged local and petty persecution, the second saw official and state persecution at hand. Others take it that, as the Epistle was about to be despatched, Peter received news of impending trouble in the area to which he wrote, and added iv. 12 ff. as a postscript.[2]

While the note of urgency in iv. 12 cannot be ignored, the difference between the sets of passages has been greatly exaggerated. For one thing, precisely similar language is used in both: if there is a 'fiery ordeal' which is a trial (*peirasmos*) in iv. 12, the trials (*peirasmoi*) of i. 6 f. are like a goldsmith's fire. In each the persecution is a ground of rejoicing (i. 6, iv. 13): the same beatitude of the Lord's is applied in each section (iii. 14, iv. 14). The glory of suffering for doing good is proclaimed in one part (iii. 17); the glory of suffering as a Christian in the other (iv. 16). We might add that in each part of the Epistle, obedience to the civil power in all things lawful and honest is strictly enjoined (ii. 13 ff., iv. 15), and in each case the implication is that the enemies of Christians would be glad of any 'handle' against them that wrong or indiscreet conduct would

---

[1] Some have even suggested a different author.
[2] Selwyn describes this surmise as 'not unreasonable' (p. 54).

provide. In each case, the example of Christ's sufferings is set forth (i. 11, iii. 18, iv. 13); and in each case the undeserved suffering of Christians is linked with the will of God (iii. 17, iv. 19). Moreover, the sufferers are bidden not to regard the *purōsis* as surprising; in the nature of things it was to be expected. This surely implies the *purōsis* was of the same nature as the sufferings spoken of earlier.

In the light of all this, it is difficult to imagine that any significant interval of time elapsed between the two parts of the Epistle, or that the persecution which is imminent in iv. 12 is substantially different from what is envisaged earlier. Suffering these people already knew (i. 6 ff.). The new peril is new only in degree, not in kind. Formally, iv. 12–v. 11 is best treated as a recapitulation of what has gone before, strongly reinforcing its principal lessons. As we have seen, some elements of the common catechetical form are repeated in this section, though occurring in their regular place earlier.[1]

c. *The nature of the persecution envisaged*[2]

In the first passage there is nothing to indicate that the 'manifold temptations' are anything other than private: though they are obviously severe. In iii. 15 ff., again the main danger seems to be from neighbours rather than the state, for the Christian has to be ready to meet enquiry on his faith (verse 15); but the section might also apply to trouble by magistrates. The phrase 'if the will of God be so' indicates at least that, though particular suffering might ensue, it was not at that time government policy automatically to attack Christians; and verse 13, like ii. 14, implies that, in the ordinary administration of justice, Christians had nothing to fear. Clearly, however, the same passage allows that the administration of justice might become extraordinary, blind and partial.

---

[1] The fourth element, however, resistance to the devil, is not found in the earlier part: a further suggestion that iv. 12 ff. is not a separate entity, but integral to the book from the beginning.

[2] On the meaning conveyed by the various terms, cf. the valuable article by Selwyn 'The Persecutions in 1 Peter', *Bulletin of Studiorum Novi Testamenti Societas*, I, 1950, pp. 39 ff.

I PETER

The passage in iv. 12 ff. contains an antithesis between suffering for wrongs committed and suffering for the name of Christ. It is peculiarly the function of the state to administer suffering for crime, which might lead one to assume that the 'suffering for the name' was to be set on foot from the same direction. Moreover, in the correspondence of Pliny, governor of Bithynia from AD 110, there occurs the question whether 'the name itself' (*nomen ipsum*) of Christian is a criminal offence, or only the 'crimes congruent therewith' (*flagitia cohaerentia*). Such a question occurring in the very area to which the letter is addressed has led many scholars to identify the persecution 'for the name' alluded to in 1 Peter, with Pliny's inquisition of AD 111.[1] But we must not be betrayed by the attractiveness of this equation into forgetting the great prominence of 'the name' of Jesus in primitive Christian thought.

In the Gospels, our Lord predicts harsh treatment for His followers for the sake of His name;[2] and preaching (false or true), healing, hospitality are in His name.[3] In the Jerusalem church, salvation, baptism, teaching, healing, are in His name;[4] and, in a very real sense, so is persecution.[5] With much of this, as we have already seen, Luke associates Peter, and it is of Peter himself, with John, that he writes, 'and they departed from the presence of the council, rejoicing that they were counted worthy to suffer shame *for his name*'.

Such thoughts would be uppermost in Christian minds as they faced the obloquy and affliction which was their regular lot. When our Epistle speaks of Christians sharing in the sufferings of Christ it witnesses to the fact that persecution is still, as it were, meted out to Christ Himself. His people receive it 'in his name', 'for his sake'.[6]

---

[1] So, e.g., Perdelwitz, Beare and others. B. H. Streeter, *The Primitive Church*, 1929, p. 128, suggests that the work, originally written in two parts about AD 90, was given its opening and closing verses in Pontus in Pliny's time.

[2] Mk. xiii. 13 and parallels, Lk. xxi. 12.

[3] E.g. Mk. ix. 37–41 (four separate occurrences).

[4] E.g. Acts ii. 21, 38, iii. 6, 16, iv. 12, 17 f., 30, v. 28.

[5] Acts v. 41, ix. 16.

[6] Cf. Acts ix. 4–5. Cf. also Mt. v. 11, the beatitude twice alluded to in the persecution passages in 1 Peter.

Such was the background of 'the name' for them. What the Roman governor said is largely coincidental. It is reproach, not execution, which is the regular part of the 'fiery trial'.[1] Whether at the hands of neighbours or mobs or local magistrates; whatever the formal charges, or whether in fact there were any, the victims were suffering because they were Christians, and hence 'for the name'.

We should observe, too, the difference of Pliny's *flagitia cohaerentia* from the sins which Peter urges Christians to repudiate. Pliny has doubtless in mind the common pagan slander that the Christians were guilty of odious crimes—incest, cannibalism and the like—in their secret rites. He is slightly puzzled that, even after torture, he can get no account from Christians of these crimes. The reason was, of course, that they did not exist. Against this sort of charge there was no adequate defence. But Peter's warnings in iv. 15 have no such undertones.[2] Indeed one of the characters in which a Christian must not appear, 'an evil-doer', is very generally expressed; and another, 'a busybody', is not a criminal offence at all. Peter's concern is solely that Christians should be, in the eyes of pagans with or without authority, blameless. Suffering mattered not, provided it was undeserved.

The final reference to persecution is important in that it indicates that the suffering of those addressed was not confined to their area, but was the common lot of contemporary Christians.

We may conclude, therefore, that 1 Peter relates to a church that is suffering as New Testament Christians invariably did suffer. As in the Acts, their major trials come from unofficial or semi-official sources, or official sources acting *ultra vires*. It is not likely that death was the regular outcome of their endur-

---

[1] 1 Pet. iv. 14.
[2] It is only fair to use the oath of abstention from crime, to which Pliny alludes, as evidence of a connection with 1 Peter iv, if one is prepared to say that it was about Pliny's time that Christians began to regard such abstention as obligatory. See W. M. Ramsay, *The Church in the Roman Empire*, 7th edn., 1903, p. 289.

ance.[1] They believed they were persecuted 'for the name', but they used that expression in a primitive Christian, and not in a juristic Roman sense.

d. *The historical background of the persecutions in 1 Peter*

In the book of Acts the Christian missionaries are in frequent trouble and perilous situations, but the persecution they meet is local, due usually to Jewish influence or to the offending of commercial interests,[2] and when a charge is preferred it does not usually bear examination.[3] The first persecution, actually set on foot by the Roman State, of which we have any certain knowledge, is that of Nero, who used the Christians as a scapegoat for the Fire of Rome,[4] AD 64. Through him Peter and Paul lost their lives.[5] There is no certain evidence that the persecution extended beyond Rome,[6] but Roman provincial governors tended to reflect the Emperor's will, and especially in any place where powerful elements were ill-disposed to Christianity there might well be a severe outbreak.[7]

We have very little precise information for the succeeding years. Sir William Ramsay believed that a nervous government regarded Christians as an actual or potential menace to security,[8] and instituted regular proceedings against them: so that from the time of Vespasian onwards, 'the name' in a tech-

---

[1] Selwyn (*art. cit.*) and W. C. van Unnik, 'The Teaching of Good Works in 1 Peter', *NTS*, I, 1955, pp. 92 ff., both assert strongly that Peter does not refer to the death of Christians, only to their sufferings. But in fairness we should remember that he uses the same word of the sufferings of Christ, which involved His death. Certainly, however, it is reproach (iv. 14) and slander (iii. 16) which he particularly mentions.

[2] E.g. Acts xvi. 19 ff., xix. 23 ff.

[3] 2 Cor. xi. 23 ff. shows that the half has not been told.

[4] Tacitus, *Annals*, xv. 44. It is virtually certain that when Tacitus says 'those who confessed' were put on trial, he means 'confessed to being Christians'.

[5] 1 Clement 5. We need not infer, however, that they suffered together (see below p. 67).

[6] Unless, with Hort, the Revelation is dated in the sixties: *The Apocalypse of St. John*, 1908, pp. xxvi ff.

[7] Cf. W. M. Ramsay, *op. cit.*, p. 245.

[8] According to Tacitus (*loc. cit.*) Christians were prosecuted under Nero, and with public approval, for 'hatred of the human race'.

nical sense was a criminal offence; it was illegal to be a Christian. Certainly the fury of the ill-starred Domitian burst out against them in AD 95, and the Revelation, which is usually dated within Domitian's reign, indicates that the persecution reached the provinces. But the most interesting pagan document on the treatment of Christians is the correspondence already referred to between Pliny, who became Governor of Bithynia in AD 110/111, and his Emperor Trajan.[1]

Pliny, who has never had to deal with Christians before, asks whether age, sex or recantation is to be allowed for in prescribing punishment. He asks also if the name of Christian itself is sufficient reason for punishment, or only the crimes of which Christians were (putatively) guilty.

His own line of conduct had been to enquire whether people were Christians: to give them the opportunity to sacrifice to the Emperor's genius: and, if they refused, to execute them for contumacy. Others were released. Neither from these apostates—some of whom said they had ceased to be Christians as long as twenty years before—nor from two Christian girls whom he tortured, could he find anything particularly reprehensible, beyond a faintly disgusting superstition.

The Christians were very numerous, found in every rank of society in city and village, and included Roman citizens. Temples of the gods had been in danger of desertion until his vigorous action. A list of names had been sent to him anonymously:[2] and there is a hint that vested interests had been hit by Christian success.[3] Trajan's reply generally approves this line of conduct. Christians are not to be sought out: if they are regularly accused, and refuse to recant, they are to be punished, but no anonymous evidence is to be admitted.

The question now arises whether 1 Peter fits into this background. We have seen that there is, on careful examination, little to connect 1 Peter with Pliny's inquisition. There are

---

[1] *Epistulae ad Traianum*, xcvi, xcvii (in some editions xcvii, xcviii).

[2] Which included names of people who denied being Christians or said they had ceased to be: perhaps a device to pay off old scores.

[3] Otherwise, the concluding note about the falling market for fodder for sacrificial victims is rather anti-climactic.

also positive factors which work against any connection. Pliny was a provincial governor, and Bithynia-Pontus was his sphere of jurisdiction. There is no suggestion that his policy was enforced in the other areas to which 1 Peter is addressed. Again v. 9 shows that their sufferings are the same in kind as those of Christians elsewhere: and unless we assume a world-wide persecution by Trajan, for which there is no evidence, this does not fit the situation.

If we look to Domitian's reign, or, like Ramsay, to a date in the seventies or eighties, we move into a sphere where we have next to no comparative evidence. If this makes a hypothesis easier to hold, it doubles the duty of explaining its necessity. Undoubtedly the main factor which has led in this direction has been the belief that 'suffering for the name' implies official action for which no warrant can be found within the usually agreed limit of Peter's lifetime. This we have sought to show is not the case. Ramsay, who held the date in Pliny's governorship to be hopelessly late, is certainly justified in holding that the action of Trajan and Pliny has its origins long in the past: it is not, as defenders of the Trajanic date sometimes imply, a new departure. Pliny, though he is unsure of the technicalities, is sure that legal action is to be taken against Christians: so, evidently, were the people who brought the accusations. But one fancies that the whole question of the *nomen ipsum* has been a false trail as far as 1 Peter is concerned. Strictly speaking, Pliny does not receive a straight answer to his question on that subject: and, strictly speaking, even he does not execute Christians for the *nomen ipsum*—he executes them for contumacy. Trajan's reply is an *ad hoc* judgment, and a most unsatisfactory one. Is 'the name' a crime or is it not? Christian profession may carry the death penalty, but the onus is on private prosecutors to bring a case, not on the governor or the police. In this way did a mainly just and humane Emperor, who suspected even the creation of a fire brigade as a potential nursery of sedition,[1] endeavour not so much to stamp out Christianity as to keep it under control. And in this unsatis-

---

[1] Pliny, *Epistulae ad Traianum*, xxxiii–xxxiv (or xlii–xliii).

factory condition, at the mercy of ill-disposed neighbours and malicious gossips, with ill-defined charges and the law in a state of deliberate vagueness, Christians had undoubtedly lived for decades. The implicit question posed by Acts, Of what offence were these men guilty?, was never clearly answered in the first century or the second.

It would seem, then, that the sufferings alluded to in 1 Peter have no special connection with any particular legislation. The trials are common to first-century Christians. How severe these could be can be seen from the whole narrative of Acts, and from other letters addressed to the 'brethren that are in the world': Thessalonians, for instance, or Hebrews, of which the first certainly, and the second probably, have no connection with any of the movements of persecution known to us.

Nothing in the conditions described demands a date later than the sixties: and if we detect a note of unusual urgency in iv. 12 ff., it may well be that in the execution of Paul, and the first rumblings of the anti-Christian pogrom that was to become the bloodbath of Nero's persecution, Peter saw a movement of the adversary that could have serious repercussions in the provinces.

'The general ordeal (*purōsis*) lay in the complete lack of security which exposed Christians at any moment, and in any part of the empire, to slander, defamation of character, boycott, mob-violence and even death: they were, or at any time or place might be, hated of all men for Christ's sake: society was inhospitable and the world unjust.'[1]

Living themselves under the strictest instructions to maintain good order and respect for properly constituted authority, constantly exhorted to good deeds and blameless life, they were social misfits. Their companions thought it strange that they no longer participated in the riotous conventionalities of Hellenistic society;[2] scandal was heaped upon them.[3] They were credited with 'hatred of the human race'. As time went on, especially as numbers increased, the suspicion took a darker hue, and they were regarded as not only un-social, but

---

[1] Selwyn, p. 54. [2] iv. 4. [3] iii. 16.

anti-social—a menace to order and society. At such times violence might overwhelm a community like the eruption of a desolating volcano. They were hated of all men—for the sake of 'the name'.

XIII. THE FORM OF I PETER

It has been observed that 1 Peter iv. 11 reaches a climax, whereafter some of the themes previously expounded are taken up anew. This verse has seemed to many a natural division of the Epistle, and to indicate that a letter has been added to a sermon, or perhaps that two letters have been welded together. Professor C. F. D. Moule has recently made the interesting suggestion that two letters, with overlapping subject-matter, were written at one time, one (i. 1–iv. 1 with a closing greeting) addressed to parts where persecution was severe, the other (i. 1–ii. 10, iv. 12–v. 14) to other parts where it was still only a possibility. The two 'insets' were then copied together.[1] One would expect such a process, however, to leave marks of textual disturbance, which is not the case. On the whole it is better to see iv. 12–v. 11 as simply recapitulating and emphasizing important elements in the exhortation.

The major section of the book has often been classed as a sermon, and no-one can fail to hear the authentic tones of the preacher within it. It is rich exhortation, rhythmically phrased, throughout. We need not suppose, however, that it has been artificially pressed into letter form in days when it was fashionable to do this.[2] Of course, there is no reason, as Mr. Cranfield suggests, why Peter himself should not have preached a sermon and later sent it as a letter, perhaps with the help of Silvanus.[3] In any case, behind every one of the New Testament writings lies a multitude of apostolic sermons.

But some features have attracted particular attention. Dibelius is struck by 'a multitude of liturgical expressions'

[1] 'The Nature and Purpose of 1 Peter', *NTS*, III, 1957, pp. 1 ff.
[2] Cf. R. L. Archer, 'The Epistolary Form in the New Testament', *Expository Times*, LXIII, 1952, pp. 296 ff.
[3] Cranfield, p. 11.

which he can explain only by setting the book in the context of public worship.[1] Perdelwitz, whose theory of the mystery religions we have noticed, saw the great theme of the book as Christian baptism, superior to all the mysteries of the heathen. B. H. Streeter[2] adopted this, and read 1 Peter as a baptismal sermon by Aristion, Bishop of Smyrna,[3] to candidates for baptism who included slaves, married women, and married men.

This theory has been taken further by H. Preisker in some brief but pregnant notes attached to his edition of the commentary of Windisch.[4] The section i. 3–iv. 11 is not so much a baptismal sermon as a liturgy, with the rubrics omitted. The feature of this interpretation is that we follow the pattern of a baptismal service from the opening prayer, with its stress on the certainties of salvation, through the instruction, to the actual baptism, which Preisker sees as occurring between i. 21 and i. 22, where the tense suddenly changes, 'having purified your souls'. Exhortations, hymns, a revelation through a prophet, a closing prayer, follow. Even then we are not finished, for we find that iv. 12 ff. is a closing service for the whole congregation: hence the persecutions, in the future for the baptismal candidates, are spoken of as present realities. Stylistic differences indicate prophets or charismatics taking part in the service.

Behind this theory lies an elaborate analysis of forms, and to many it will appear rather too elaborate. What criteria have we, for instance, by which to recognize a 'revelation'?[5] Are we justified in isolating a closing prayer while admitting that it is not now at all in prayer form?[6] Those who are attracted by the

---

[1] Dibelius, p. 187.
[2] *The Primitive Church*, 1929, pp. 115 ff. Streeter knew the work of Perdelwitz only at second-hand, and does not employ his theory of the mystery religion contacts.
[3] One of the many breath-taking suggestions in this intriguing, but often wayward, book.
[4] *Die Katholischen Briefe* in Lietzmann's *Handbuch zum Neuen Testament*, 3rd edn., Tubingen, 1951. The relevant section is on pp. 156 ff.
[5] Preisker finds one in iii. 13–iv. 7a (Windisch, p. 158).
[6] Preisker sees iv. 7b–11 as a closing prayer, but cast into epistolary form (Windisch, p. 159).

theory point to the frequent use of 'now'[1] as indicating that a rite is in progress: but they might more appropriately be taken as an example of the exultant sense of the last times which rings like a bell through the Epistle.[2]

Nor are the references to our being 'begotten again unto a lively hope'[3] or the exhortations to desire milk as new-born babes[4] sure evidence that a baptism is in progress. The act of begetting is already realized and its result enjoyed: it cannot refer to an event to take place after i. 21. The phrase leads us to look at its corresponding member in the catechetical form preserved in James where the reference is quite clear: 'Of his own will begat he us with the word of truth, that we should be a kind of firstfruits of his creatures.'[5] In both Peter and James, the 'begetting' relates to the word of the gospel, rather than to the waters of baptism. This is confirmed by i. 23, on Preisker's view part of the baptismal dedication, where the recipients are described as 'born again . . . by the word of God', later explicitly defined as the enduring gospel preached to them.[6]

The figure of babes and milk is too common in the New Testament to demand a special significance here.[7] Indeed, though Professor Moule may be right in saying that the 'pattern' of baptism is much in the author's mind, it may be worth noting that the one place in the Epistle which contains an explicit reference to baptism is a parenthesis.[8]

---

[1] i. 6, 8, 12, ii. 10, 25, iii. 21.

[2] Cf. E. G. Selwyn, 'Eschatology in 1 Peter' in *The Background of the New Testament and its Eschatology*, edited by W. D. Davies and D. Daube, Cambridge, 1956, pp. 394 f. 'This "now" is an important feature of the epistle . . . not to be confined to the moment of conversion or of baptism, but indicating a period and a situation when the new Israel comprising both Jew and Gentile had been brought into being and the tide of the universal Gospel was felt to be in full flood.'

The word 'now' in iii. 21, while occurring in the same context as baptism, surely only points a contrast with the ancient flood.

[3] i. 3; cf. i. 23.   [4] ii. 2.

[5] Jas. i. 18.

[6] Surely *not* the baptismal formula? (So Cross, p. 34.)

[7] Cf. Mt. xi. 25; Lk. x. 21; 1 Cor. iii. 1, 2; 1 Thes. ii. 7 (TR); Heb. v. 12, 13. The use of *brephos* in 1 Pet. ii. 2 as against *nēpios* in the other cases quoted is not likely to be significant.

[8] iii. 21.

The hypothesis has been transfigured by Professor Cross in the monograph already mentioned, in which he sustains most attractively, and with characteristic wealth of patristic learning, the thesis that 1 Peter is the celebrant's part for a baptismal service held on Easter Day. He points to the constant use of *paschein*, 'to suffer', in the Epistle, where it is far more frequent than anywhere else in the New Testament, and suggests a word-play, for which there is abundant parallel, with *Pascha*, Easter.[1] He traces the Exodus typology through 1 Peter. The Epistle's themes may be summed up thus: 'Baptism, Passover, Passion-Resurrection, moral duties.' 'The one setting where these subjects belong together' is the Paschal Baptismal Eucharist.[2]

Dr. Cross points to a number of details from early Christian sources (and clearly he has others in reserve) and principally the *Apostolic Tradition* of Hippolytus, written in Rome about AD 215, but undoubtedly containing much earlier material. These details, he holds, shed untold light upon what is happening in 1 Peter. He invites those who will to follow him in the full comparative study of 1 Peter with the baptismal and confirmation rite in the *Apostolic Tradition*.[3]

The invitation will undoubtedly be widely accepted.[4] No

---

[1] In the examples of this word-play cited by Dr. Cross, however, *both* the words *Pascha* and some form of *paschein* occur: in 1 Peter we have only the latter. Moreover, as Dr. W. C. van Unnik puts it, 'The use of the Greek verb *pascho*, to suffer, is so closely linked up with current facts that it never suggests a word play with *Pascha*—Easter'. ('Christianity according to 1 Peter', *Expository Times*, LXVIII, 1956, pp. 79 ff.)   [2] Cross, p. 36.

[3] Dr. Cross submits this analysis:

i. 3–12	The Bishop's solemn opening prayer.
i. 13–21	His formal charge to the candidates.
i. 22–25	(The baptism having taken place) The Bishop's welcome of the newly baptized.
ii. 1–10	The Bishop on the fundamentals of sacramental life.
ii. 11–iv. 6	The Bishop's address on Christian duties.
iv. 7–11	Final admonitions and doxology.

Dr. Cross uses the term 'Bishop', as he says, 'without prejudice'.

[4] Dr. Beare warmly welcomes the hypothesis (2nd edn., pp. 200 ff.). 'I do not see how anyone can fail to see that there is a certain, even a marked degree of formal relationship.' It is criticized by Professor Moule (*NTS*, III, 1957, pp. 1 ff.) and, more cursorily, by Professor van Unnik (*Expository Times*, LXVIII, 1956, pp. 79 ff.).

source must be neglected that may shed light upon the sacred text. Certain caveats must, however, be kept in mind. In the first place, any reserve we feel about Preisker's hypothesis will necessarily attach to this new form of it.[1] Again, it will be possible in the nature of the study to read too easily into our texts ideas exterior to them. (For instance, it must be remembered that, however likely we may think it, the *Apostolic Tradition* does not actually say that the baptism took place at Easter;[2] and there may be traces of Exodus typology that have no connection with either Easter or baptism.[3]) *The Apostolic Tradition*, too, is a work packed with problems, textual, historical and liturgical. It is not always safe to assume that we know what Hippolytus wrote; or if we do, that in every case he represents Rome, or indeed anyone but himself: for *Apostolic Tradition* is essentially a polemical work.[4] And even where we may find a correspondence in some later document which appears to light up I Peter, we must be prepared for I Peter to make sense without this.[5]

[1] Dr. Cross removes the element of hypercriticism from Preisker's stylistic and formal divisions.

[2] G. Dix, in his edition, supplies rubrics and section headings which imply that the rite took place in Holy Week, but these are not part of the text as it has come down. Hippolytus indicates (ed. Dix, xx. 7) that the baptism should take place on Sunday, but he does not define more closely. He deals with the Easter fast much later (xxix).

[3] E.g. xxviii. 6. A suggestion on these lines is made by A. F. Walls, 'A Primitive Christian Harvest Thanksgiving', *Theology*, LVIII, 1955, pp. 336 ff.

[4] There is no text of the *Apostolic Tradition* as such; it survives in a very fragmentary (and probably modified) Latin translation, and has been incorporated to varying degrees in works in Greek, Syriac, Coptic, Arabic and Ethiopic. Though he lived in Rome, Hippolytus came from an Eastern church tradition, and there is much evidence of the effect of this on his work, which purports to instruct true believers on the proper and 'apostolic' rule of church government, liturgy and practice. Either slightly before or slightly after writing the work he seems to have broken with the Roman church.

[5] Space forbids the proper discussion of examples: but Professor van Unnik can say, 'Many expressions which Dr. Cross connects with baptism have a far more general meaning' (*art. cit.*, p. 80). ii. 2, it has been suggested, is illuminated by the cup of milk and honey given to newly-baptized persons at first communion (*Ap. Trad.*, xxiii. 2). But only milk is mentioned, the milk of Christian nourishment, whereas in the custom to which patristic

If we restrict ourselves to what can be averred with confidence, we know that 1 Peter reaches us as a letter; and as a letter we must primarily study it.[1] And if we read it as a letter, the prominence given to baptism is less marked than might be expected from contemporary discussions.

XIV. THE DESTINATION OF THE EPISTLE

The letter is addressed to the Christians of Pontus, Galatia, Cappadocia, Asia and Bithynia.[2] If we take the strict boundaries of those provinces, most of Asia Minor—all of it north of the Taurus Mountains—would be included. But we are probably not to do so. Throughout the period to which 1 Peter has been ascribed, the provinces of Bithynia and Pontus were merged for administrative purposes, yet Peter mentions them separately. We are obliged to think therefore that he does not necessarily refer strictly to Roman political boundaries.

In that case, it becomes significant that both 'Asia' and 'Galatia' were used popularly in a more limited sense than their political connotation. Thus 'Galatia' could mean North Galatia, or Galatia proper, and three separate parts of Asia were called by the provincial name.

In Acts xvi. 6, 7, Paul and his companions are forbidden by the Holy Spirit to preach in 'Asia'—used here in a restricted sense—and Bithynia. Was the reason that Peter, among others, was already labouring in these areas? If so, it is probable that the more restricted sense of Asia and Galatia is

writers refer the honey is essential to the symbolism: it is the promised land which the new Christian has entered. Interestingly enough, Perdelwitz (*op. cit.*, pp. 56 ff.) quotes a string of pagan analogies which he believes illustrate the verse.

[1] Nor is it easy to explain why a liturgical text should be converted into a letter. Cf. Moule, *art. cit.*, p. 4: 'I do not find it easy . . . to conceive how a liturgy-homily shorn of its "rubrics" (which, of course, were probably oral), but with its changing tenses and broken sequences all retained, could have been hastily dressed up as a letter and sent off (without a word of explanation) to Christians who had not witnessed its original setting.'

[2] It is arbitrary to disregard the address as a device and assume that it is a 'General Epistle' to the whole Church, because it is hard to make out the personal circumstances of sender and recipients—so Dibelius, pp. 187 f.

intended here. The area addressed is much reduced by this proposal but it has an important element of homogeneity—it is, broadly speaking, the whole of Asia Minor that was not evangelized by Paul.[1]

The order of naming is, however, curious. It is not alphabetical, it is not the order in which the provinces would be visualized from any of the likely places of writing. Pontus and Bithynia, which are parts of one province, occur respectively first and last. W. L. Knox has urged that the order is simply for good rhythmic effect.[2] Beare, who holds that those persecuted by Pliny are addressed, is forced to the rather precarious suggestion that Pontus and Bithynia are placed at the beginning and end of the list for prominence, since it was in those areas that persecution was rampant; and the other provinces, where we have no such evidence, are placed between, as the persecution might spread there.[3] The old suggestion of Hort has not yet been bettered. 'If . . . the indicated order is not that of a distant prospect in imagination, but of an actual intended journey, it answers precisely . . . to a course which would naturally be followed by one landing at a seaport of Pontus, making a circuit through the principal known or probable seats of Christian communities, and returning to the neighbourhood of the Euxine.'[4]

And the messenger following that route may well have been Silvanus himself.

XV. THE PLACE OF WRITING

1 Peter is addressed from Babylon. There are two places of that

---

[1] This assumes that the Galatians to whom Paul's letter was addressed were South Galatians.

[2] In a review of Selwyn, *Theology*, XLIX, 1946, p. 344.

[3] Beare, pp. 23 f.

[4] F. J. A. Hort, *The First Epistle of St. Peter*, 1898, p. 15. Beare's objection that no messenger could plan his itinerary if a fierce anti-Christian persecution was in progress only has force on his own view that the letter belongs to Pliny's time in Pontus. Silvanus might have reached these communities with at least the certainty of Timothy reaching the persecuted Thessalonians (1 Thes. iii. 2). Nor would the use of a messenger, the personal envoy of the apostle and a man of high repute himself, necessarily mean that there would be only one copy of the letter. Silvanus was not simply coming as a postman.

name. The ancient city of Mesopotamia, an area which was then a centre of pure and uncompromising Judaism, might conceivably have a claim on the apostle of the circumcision.[1] It seems too much of a coincidence, however, that Mark and Silvanus, Paul's companions, should be there, too: and the fact that the Eastern Church made no attempt to claim the apostle for itself until quite late, and then only on the basis of this passage, indicates that no tradition of Peter's sojourn took root there.

There was also a Roman frontier post on the Nile, called Babylon from its reputed origination from Babylonian rebels.[2] In favour of an Egyptian sojourn for Peter one might cite— though hardly with confidence—the well-known connection of Mark with the Alexandrine Church, and the fact that Basilides, an Alexandrine heretic, claimed to hold Peter's apostolic tradition through his interpreter Glaukias.[3] But Babylon was hardly more than a fortress, and there seems no particular reason why Peter should make his base there.[4]

It is far more likely that 'Babylon' stands for Rome. We find it used in the Apocalypse with this signification:[5] and, bearing in mind that the way was already prepared in the Old Testament,[6] its use as a code-word[7] among Christians is readily intelligible. The submissive attitude to the Roman state in I Peter is not, as is sometimes alleged, an obstacle to this: for more than persecution made Rome the mother of harlots. Rome explains the presence of Mark: and we have every reason to believe that Peter worked there.

Beare now accepts Rome as the place of writing, having been convinced through Dr. Cross's work of the connection of

---

[1] There are Jews from Persia and Mesopotamia in the Pentecost crowd (Acts ii. 9).

[2] Strabo, *Geography*, XVII, 1.30.

[3] Clement of Alexandria, *Stromateis*, vii. 17.

[4] The case for this Babylon is argued by G. T. Manley, 'Babylon on the Nile', *Evangelical Quarterly*, XVI, 1944, pp. 138 ff.

[5] Rev. xiv. 8, xvii. 5, etc.

[6] E.g. Is. xiv.

[7] Some (e.g. Selwyn) think of it as a cryptogram for security purposes, but this would be hardly necessary in such a letter as I Peter.

1 Peter with Hippolytus and thus with the Roman liturgy.[1] Previously he had held, like others maintaining a late date, that the name Babylon, though meant to be understood as Rome, conveyed no real information, as the book was written in the area for which it was intended.[2] A recent variation of this suggests that 'Babylon' is merely intended as a designation of the place of exile, as opposed to the heavenly country, recalling 'the dispersion' in i. 1.[3] But this leaves vague a reference one expects to be specific; the *whole church* was in this sense 'in Babylon': Peter is conveying the greetings of a particular church.

XVI. THE DATE OF THE EPISTLE

The Epistle is usually dated in one of three periods, in the reign of Trajan, *c.* AD 111, a little before or after:[4] in or about the reign of Domitian, *c.* AD 90–100: or in the reign of Nero, *c.* AD 62–64. To these we must add the view of Sir William Ramsay, an army in himself, who held a date *c.* AD 80. He was influenced in this partly by his theory about persecution for the name, and partly because he was convinced that Pontus could not have been evangelized before that date to the extent presupposed by the Epistle. Despite his formidable judgment in such matters, neither supposition is safe ground, and his extension of Peter's life to the date he supposed for the book is quite baseless.

If the arguments so far advanced are sound, a date AD 80–100 is not demanded for our book, and a date after that is impossible.

[1] Though Hippolytus is a rather dubious witness for Roman liturgy (as Beare seems to half-acknowledge in his reference to a Syrian background for *Apostolic Tradition*: 2nd edn., p. 204).

[2] Streeter believed that the work had been written in Asia, but the address added in Bithynia-Pontus, when the relevance of the book was discovered in the persecution there.

[3] So M. E. Boismard, 'Une Liturgie Baptismale dans le Prima Petri', II, *RB*, LXIV, 1957, p. 181. P. Boismard finds the origin of the book in Antioch: he sees a baptismal liturgy in it which left its marks elsewhere.

[4] Older commentators frequently raised the date to AD 115 or even later, but this is no longer proposed. Every additional year makes the external evidence more embarrassing.

The most satisfactory date is a little before the outbreak of the Neronian persecution, in AD 63 or early 64.[1] Perhaps the murder of James the Just in Jerusalem in AD 62, as Selwyn suggests, with its implicit final repudiation of Christianity by Judaism, would give the Galilean apostle's address to his Gentile brethren, 'elect sojourners of the dispersion', a particular poignancy.[2] Or perhaps we should date the letter after the death of Paul, whose companions, Mark and Silvanus, now turned to aid Peter, and became the writers of Peter's Gospel and the writer of Peter's Epistle respectively.[3] We cannot know the circumstances: except that within eighteen months, or at the utmost two years after writing this letter, Peter followed James and Paul in drinking the cup of the sufferings and the glory to the full.

XVII. THE AUTHOR AND HIS MESSAGE

We have touched in the preceding pages on many aspects of the Epistle and its writing. To many these things point irresistibly in one direction: this is not only the apostolic doctrine, to which the Spirit bears witness; this is the very work of Christ's apostle.

That the prophet Silvanus was also concerned, is highly probable. The precise relation between them in the production of the Epistle will never be known to us. It is bound to be beyond the wit of a later generation to disentangle strands woven through the harmony of creative men used to working together. Nor, were it possible, would it be greatly profitable. As the Epistle comes to us, it comes under the signature and with the authority of Peter, apostle of Jesus Christ and witness

[1] The fact that, as a general principle, the government may be expected to administer justice (ii. 13 ff.) and a man who does good be unmolested (iii. 13), leads one to think of a time before the persecution in Rome was under way. But Selwyn (*Bulletin of Studiorum Novi Testamenti Societas*, I, 1950, pp. 49 f.), citing W. L. Knox, points out that in 1 Clement, written under the shadow of Domitian's persecution, there is a similar meekness of expression about the authorities.
[2] Selwyn, pp. 56 ff.
[3] Cf. F. Warburton Lewis, 'Note on the Date of the First Epistle of Peter', *Expositor*, 5th series, vol. X, 1899, pp. 319 ff.

of his sufferings and glory. And as the Christian reader pursues it, he cannot stop at its haunting rhythms. The voice of the one who boasted and blustered and denied his Lord; who, as the Lord looked on him, went out and wept bitterly; who rejoiced that he was counted worthy to suffer shame for His sake, and who stretched forth his hands to glorify God in his death; who modestly calls himself 'fellow-elder and witness'; the voice of such a man, who knew the full heat of the furnace in which Christian faith is tried, arrests him, and points him to his Servant-Saviour. And perhaps he may pray:

> Ah! show me that happiest place,
> The place of Thy people's abode,
> Where saints in an ecstasy gaze,
> And hang on a crucified God;
> Thy love for a sinner declare,
> Thy passion and death on the tree;
> My spirit to Calvary bear,
> To suffer and triumph with Thee.

ANALYSIS

I. OPENING SALUTATION (i. 1, 2).

II. THE CHARACTER OF OUR GOD-WROUGHT SALVATION (i. 3–12).

III. THE CHALLENGE TO LIVE DIFFERENTLY (i. 13–ii. 3).
   a. God's purpose for His elect (i. 13–16).
   b. A call to the redeemed to fear God (i. 17–21).
   c. Expressing the new life (i. 22–ii. 3).

IV. THE PRIVILEGES OF BELONGING TO THE PEOPLE OF GOD (ii. 4–10).
   a. The new 'spiritual house' (ii. 4, 5).
   b. The chief cornerstone (ii. 6–8).
   c. The people of God (ii. 9, 10).

V. CHRISTIAN LIVING IN RELATION TO OTHERS (ii. 11–iii. 12).
   a. Some reasons for self-discipline (ii. 11, 12).
   b. The duty of submission to the secular power (ii. 13–17).
   c. The duty of servants to masters (ii. 18–21a).
   d. The example of Christ our Redeemer (ii. 21b–25).
   e. The duties of wives and husbands (iii. 1–7).
   f. Principles of Christian living (iii. 8–12).

VI. SUFFERING FOR RIGHTEOUSNESS' SAKE (iii. 13–17).

VII. CHRIST'S SUFFERING AND ITS TRIUMPHANT CONSEQUENCES (iii. 18–22).

VIII. A FURTHER CALL TO HOLY LIVING (iv. 1–6).

IX. THE PRACTICAL DEMANDS OF CHRISTIAN DISCIPLESHIP (iv. 7–11).

I PETER

COMMENTARY

I. OPENING SALUTATION (i. 1, 2)

According to customary usage the writer of the letter names himself and his readers and expresses his goodwill towards them in greeting. This basic framework is here amplified in the description of both writer and readers by enriching Christian awareness. For both are related to Jesus Christ. Peter has His special commission as His apostle; and his readers, though temporarily scattered sojourners in various parts of Asia Minor, are all chosen of God, according to His predetermined intention and by the sanctifying work of the Spirit, to share in a new obedience to His will, and in the cleansing and the consecration which are made theirs through the sacrifice of Jesus Christ. So Peter desires that this gracious manifestation of the divine favour towards them, and the crowning blessing of peace which it bestows, may be increasingly theirs.

1. *Peter.* This is the Greek form of the name meaning 'a stone' (in Aramaic, 'Cephas'), which was given to Simon, the son of John, by our Lord (see Jn. i. 42; cf. Mt. xvi. 18). It was his distinctive Christian name. Note that in ii. 4, 5 Peter himself uses the same idea to describe all who come to Christ; they become 'as stones'. The phrase *an apostle of Jesus Christ* may convey the twofold meaning: (1) sent by Jesus Christ, (2) sent to serve and proclaim Jesus Christ. It is this commission which gives Peter authority to write such a letter to Christians. His appeal to it here is the more pertinent if he was writing to Christians with whom he had had no previous personal contact.

The 'address' indicates that the intended readers of this Epistle dwelt in the various parts of Asia Minor north of the

Taurus Mountains (see Introduction, p. 63). Peter describes them as 'sojourners of the Dispersion' (RV). The word *diaspora*, rendered 'Dispersion', was used to denote Jews living outside Palestine (see Jn. vii. 35). It is here used to describe Christians, and to suggest that in this world they are not only scattered but also away from their true homeland or metropolis in heaven. Such dwelling in this world is, therefore, only a 'sojourning' (see i. 17 where the word is *paroikia*, 'a dwelling alongside') in a place to which they do not belong. So they are here called 'sojourners', *parepidēmoi*, a word which emphasizes both alien nationality and temporary residence. It is used in Gn. xxiii. 4, LXX, of Abraham dwelling in Canaan, and in Ps. xxxix. 12 of man's sojourn on earth. Christians are thus challenged by Peter's opening address to think of themselves as citizens of heaven, and only 'strangers and pilgrims' here (cf. ii. 11).

2. In the Greek the word *elect* opens Peter's description of his readers, and indicates their relation to God, before their position in the world as 'sojourners' is described (see RV). What in the Old Testament is a characteristic of Israel (see Dt. xiv. 2; Is. xlv. 4) is here transferred to the Christian community as the new Israel (cf. ii. 9, 10). Three successive phrases follow which significantly mention the names of the three Persons of the Trinity, and indicate that They all co-operate to bring about men's participation in a heavenly destiny. Election originates in *God the Father*, in His eternal will and purpose. His *foreknowledge* includes the thought of His foreordaining (cf. i. 20; Acts ii. 23). This choice and purpose of God take effect through the activity of *the Spirit*, who deals with men in *sanctification* to set them apart and make them fit for this heavenly calling. The end in view is *obedience*—that the elect should serve the divine pleasure. Participation in such a destiny requires also the *sprinkling of the blood of Jesus Christ*. In the light of Old Testament vocabulary and usage such phraseology has more than one possible reference. It can refer to the transference to the elect of the merits and the atoning and cleansing virtue of Christ's death (cf. Nu. xix. 9; Heb. ix. 13).

It can refer to the sealing of the new covenant, and to participation in its benefits and obligations (cf. Ex. xxiv. 3–8). It can refer to consecration to priestly service, including full access to God's presence (cf. Ex. xxix. 21; Lv. viii. 30; Heb. x. 19–22). Such references may rightly all find possible inclusion here. Also, it is noteworthy that the *sprinkling of the blood* is mentioned last. This possibly suggests that the cleansing virtue of Christ's death is available, and will be needed, until the end of our earthly pilgrimage (cf. 1 Jn. i. 7). Our calling is to obey; but when we fail the atoning blood can still be sprinkled.

Grace . . . , and peace, be multiplied. Peter concludes his salutation with the prayer that his readers may increase in personal experience of the character and benefit of God's dealings with men in Christ and by the Spirit.

II. THE CHARACTER OF OUR GOD-WROUGHT SALVATION (i. 3–12)

God is here adored as the Author of an act of mercy in Christ by which we are given a sure hope of possessing a heavenly inheritance and of being brought safely to the time of its full enjoyment. This prospect should fill us with joy, even in the midst of present grievous trials, particularly when we realize that the purpose of such trials is to demonstrate the genuineness of our faith, and thus to bring greater glory to our Saviour in the day of His public manifestation. Meanwhile, too, it is possible for us to have a foretaste of the unspeakable joy of that day in our present fellowship with the unseen Lord and in our present appropriation of realized salvation. It was of this salvation that the prophets of old strove to foretell. The Spirit of Christ in them revealed that to make such grace available for men—particularly Gentile outsiders—and to bring to pass such crowning glories as are now assured for God's Christ, it was ordained that He should suffer. The prophets of old and the present preachers of the gospel are alike divinely appointed to promote our participation in this salvation. It is all so amazing that in heaven the angels peer down with wondering gaze eager to discern more.

3. *Blessed be the God.* . . . . Only in such an attitude of worship can the fulness of the truth which follows be expressed. God, the Author of our salvation, is here described in a distinctive, Christian way. The Israelites blessed God as the Creator of the world, and as their Redeemer from Egypt. Christians bless God as the Father of the incarnate Son, and as the One who raised this Jesus from the dead. Thus He is to be acknowledged as the Author of new creation and of spiritual redemption.

This Jesus is also explicitly described as *our Lord Jesus Christ*, that is, as God's promised Messiah, as the divinely exalted Lord of the universe, and as appointed by God in the discharge of these two offices to be 'ours', i.e. to discharge them in our interest and for our benefit, individually and corporately. God made this Jesus to be Lord and Christ when He raised Him from the dead (cf. Acts ii. 36). The outstanding significance of His *resurrection*, therefore, is here emphasized. That is where all our *hope* takes its rise—hope which, like the risen Lord Himself, is 'living' (RV), or undying (see Rom. vi. 9). We, too, share in this hope as 'living'; i.e. it becomes not only our expectation, but also our life, because through the same resurrection of Christ we ourselves are born or *begotten again*, and thus share in Christ's undying life.

The verb *anagennān*, 'to beget again', found here and in i. 23, is not used anywhere else in the New Testament or LXX. Its use may well have been suggested by our Lord's saying in Jn. iii. 3. There the Greek phrase is *gennēthēnai anōthen*, 'to be born or begotten again'. It first expresses a decisive change of status and prospect, wholly due to the decisive work of Christ for us (cf. ii. 24, iii. 18), a work successfully consummated in Christ's resurrection (cf. iii. 21). It further implies actual participation in new God-given life, or new birth of the Spirit (see i. 23). Of these two benefits water baptism is the outward sign and seal (cf. Tit. iii. 5). So, in later Christian writers, *anagennān* is sometimes used of baptism; and some would like to assert that it implies this here. It is dangerous thus to divert attention away from the divinely-wrought spiritual realities to the sign, whose whole *raison d'être* is to direct attention and faith to the real cause and occasion of regeneration, i.e. not the water baptism, but the death and resurrection of Christ, and the believing response of the individual to the risen Lord. This act of God in its bearing upon our salvation is here recognized as a manifestation of *his abundant mercy*. Mercy is a word specially used in the New Testament of God's kindness in bringing in the outsider and the unworthy, the Gentile and the sinner, to share in His salvation, and in the glories or riches of His Christ (see Rom. xi. 30–32, xv. 9; Eph. ii. 1–7; Tit. iii. 5).

4. What we may particularly anticipate is the possession of our promised *inheritance*. In Old Testament times this word described the appointed portion or lot to be possessed in Canaan by every one of God's people. Here it translates *klēronomia* which includes the idea of full realized possession of the inheritance rather than just the title to it. The corresponding 'reward of the inheritance' (Col. iii. 24), to which Christians may look forward in Christ, is, by contrast with that of the Israelites, not on earth but *in heaven*. Three negative compounds are strung together to indicate that, unlike any inheritance in this world, it is not exposed to destruction or defilement from outside, or to decay from inside. It cannot, like the earthly Canaan, be ravaged or polluted (see Lv. xviii. 27); nor will it ever, like earthly possessions, wear out or waste away. This inheritance has already been carefully put aside or *reserved* (a perfect participle in the Greek), and so is in consequence waiting for us to enjoy. At its highest this inheritance, thus to be possessed, is the Lord Himself (see Ps. xvi. 5, and cf. the Westminster Shorter Catechism, 'The chief end of man is . . . to enjoy Him for ever'). Those who 'seek those things which are above' (see Col. iii. 1–3) find their crowning satisfaction in the Christ who sits on the right hand of God. He is the inviolable treasure, safely deposited and permanently

enthroned in heaven for the eternal enjoyment of His people
(see Gn. xv. 1; 1 Thes. iv. 17, v. 9, 10). The further truth is
that the full possession of this inheritance will bring the complementary reward of participation in Christ's glory as the
exalted Man (see Col. iii. 4, RV). For when we shall see Him
as He is, we are to be made like Him (1 Jn. iii. 2). Such is the
character of the full 'redemption of the purchased possession',
or the complete enjoyment of the promised inheritance, which
Christ's people may now anticipate. Of this inheritance the
indwelling Spirit is the 'earnest' or first instalment. His
presence in our hearts is the guarantee of its full possession
(see Eph. i. 14; Rom. viii. 11, 18–23).

5. Not only is this wonderful, heavenly inheritance prepared
for our enjoyment, but we, for whom it is divinely intended,
are being continuously 'guarded' (RV; *phrouroumenous*, a present
participle, is a military term; cf. 2 Cor. xi. 32; Phil. iv. 7),
and so preserved, throughout the whole of our earthly pilgrimage, by nothing less than divine power, in order that we
may safely reach the goal of its full possession. Here we have
expressed the unmistakable confidence of the apostolic writers
that God Himself will see that those who are called to share in
the fulfilment of this promise of an inheritance will all safely
reach the goal of its full enjoyment (cf. Phil. i. 6; 1 Cor. i. 8).
Yet the human condition, both of continuance in the enjoyment of this divine protection, and of ultimate possession of
this divinely-prepared salvation, is equally recognized as
having its necessary place. We thus experience continual protection, and shall enter into complete salvation only *through
faith.*

The *salvation* here in view is a hope and a consummation of
the future, an eschatological fulfilment. It is something fully
prepared beforehand by God (cf. Lk. ii. 30, 31), and sure of
realization, yet still waiting to be manifested when the time is
ripe for it. (Some expositors prefer to regard the phrase *ready
to be revealed* as qualifying 'inheritance' rather than 'salvation'.
It makes little difference to the sense.) This eschatological

emphasis means that, however truly salvation may have already begun in the experience of those who believe in Christ (see Lk. xix. 9) and however much it may be a daily experience of their earthly discipleship (see 2 Cor. vi. 2), its full character and wonder will be disclosed only in the crowning day that is coming. What Christ's people then enjoy will be 'salvation' indeed (see Rom. xiii. 11 and Heb. i. 14, ix. 28 for similar use of the word).

6, 7. This assured prospect of an inheritance and this assured preservation by God's power afford ground for unceasing joy, even in the midst of possible present trials, especially when the purpose of the trials in relation to the expected consummation is realized. God allows the trials in order to find out by testing the genuine element in men's professed faith. In God's eyes such true faith is more precious than pure gold, which similarly has its genuineness tested and demonstrated by fire. For, when Jesus is publicly manifested as God's Christ for all to see, what will win His approval and reward, and bring complementary glory to Him, will be the accompanying disclosure that, in the face of the darkness and pain of earthly circumstance and opposition, His people have trusted Him as God's Christ, and proved His power to guard them and to fill them with joyful hope.

Wherein probably refers to the circumstances of divinely provided blessing just described. *For a season*, RV 'for a little while', emphasizes the short duration of all earthly trial compared with the eternal reward (cf. 2 Cor. iv. 17). *If need be* may simply recognize that such an experience is a possibility, i.e. circumstances may make it inevitable. But the word *deon* suggests a probable reference to the kind of divine necessity that Jesus Himself saw in His own sufferings. Such trials are sometimes a 'must' for God's people if His will is to be done (cf. iii. 17). *Temptations*; 'trials' (RV mg., RSV) better expresses the sense. '*Peirasmos* here means not the inner wrestling with evil inclination, but undeserved suffering from without' (Bigg).

Ye are in heaviness (RV 'ye have been put to grief') is a phrase in paradoxical opposition to *ye greatly rejoice*. There is here full, frank recognition that earthly trials cause deeply felt mental distress. Such experience is the very circumstance in which to prove also the unique character of true Christian rejoicing. For the believer whose hope is in the promised inheritance or salvation, and who recognizes that the trials are meant in God's providence to serve positive ends for Christ's glory and the Christian's spiritual profit, can actually take delight in being grieved (cf. Rom. v. 2–4, viii. 18; Jas. i. 2–4).

That translates *hina*, 'in order that'; verse 7 indicates the purpose of thus being put to grief. *The trial* (RV 'proof'; RSV 'genuineness') *of your faith*. The Greek phrase refers to the approved residue of faith, that faith whose genuineness has thus been proved by testing. Just as men use fire to distinguish true gold from counterfeit, so God uses trials to distinguish genuine faith from superficial profession. *Gold* is here used in comparison because, although it is only part of this perishable creation, it is of sufficient value, compared with other things with which it may be mixed and confused, to have its genuineness discovered and demonstrated by the test of fire. Since *faith* is in God's sight so much more precious, and has, when genuine, imperishable value, it is understandable that God should similarly use the fires of trial to discover and to demonstrate where true faith exists. So the trials of our earthly experience are not to be regarded as strange or surprising, but as providentially ordered for divine and eternal ends (cf. iv. 12).

The *praise and honour and glory* which such genuine faith will secure in the day of full disclosure will, from one standpoint, be given to the true believers by the approving Lord. From another standpoint they will be given to the Lord Himself, who is thus openly shown to have been worthy of trust by both the devotion and the experience of those who trusted Him. *At the appearing of Jesus Christ* is a reference to Christ's second advent. The use of *apokalupsis*, *appearing* (RV 'revelation'), suggests not the 'coming' of someone hitherto absent, but the visible unveiling or disclosure of someone who has been all the time spiritually and invisibly present (see also I Cor. i. 7; 2 Thes. i. 7).

8, 9. Not only is great and continuous joy possible now in the midst of trials because of the hope set before us; there are also causes of yet greater joy. These are realized fellowship with the living unseen Lord, active love for Him, and daily counting upon Him, issuing (as such faith will yet do finally and eternally) here and now in a real measure of salvation in the soul. All these give a yet greater experience of present unceasing joy (cf. Phil. iv. 4), which baffles description in words, and shares beforehand in the glory of the coming full revelation.

There is a contrast here between the sight of Jesus, possibly both at His first and at His second advents, and the knowledge of Him by faith, which is the present experience of His people. Peter's readers had not seen Jesus during His earthly life, as Peter himself had done, yet they were giving Him the responsive love of their hearts in living fellowship. They could not now see Him, as all will see Him at His appearing, yet they were continually expressing active confidence in Him, and sharing in the consequent blessing (cf. Jn. xx. 29).

The participle *pisteuontes, believing,* is in the present continuous tense. It describes a habitual or typical activity. It is accompanied by a phrase, *in whom (eis* with the accusative), expressing movement into, entrance into, or union with. Believing thus finds full expression, when, being sure of the presence and the trustworthiness of Christ, the person exercising faith comes to Jesus in self-committal, and continues actively to rest and rely upon Him (cf. Heb. xi. 6). The verb translated *ye rejoice* is expressive of such strong feeling or exultation that there is some justification for rendering it 'rejoice greatly' (as in verse 6, and as in RV here); or 'be exceeding glad' (Mt. v. 12). *Unspeakable* means unable to be expressed, incapable of declaration in words. *Full of glory*; better, 'glorified' as RV mg.; i.e. the joy is already irradiated with the glory of heaven or of the coming day of revelation.

Receiving, komizomenoi, is a present participle in the middle voice, expressing the idea of 'acquiring for oneself' in personal appropriation and enjoyment. Some think this means that true faith expresses such active appropriation or reckoning, and brings such accompanying assurance, that its future reward is as good as enjoyed already. The actual 'salvation' is thus still future, as in verse 5. Others prefer to regard the present tense of the participle as referring to an experience of salvation which is in real measure realized and enjoyed here and now. This phrase, in whichever sense it is understood, indicates the reason for the inexpressible and glorious character of the consequent joy. *The end, telos*, refers not to the cessation or conclusion, but to the goal or consummation of our faith.

It is noteworthy that Christ is said to bring into expression three fundamental, responsive activities, hope (verse 3), faith (verses 7, 9) and love (verse 8) (cf. 1 Thes. i. 3, v. 8), with joy (verse 8) added as an inevitable consequence and all centred supremely on His Person as alive from the dead. Also faith is said to have dealings in two directions—in relation to both the unseen Lord and the future hope of salvation (cf. Heb. xi. 1). These activities are characteristic and distinctive of vital Christianity.

10-12. In times past this salvation has been to divinely-inspired prophets a subject of quest and enquiry; it is continually to angels a subject of eager interest. The prophets spoke of the divine grace destined to be extended to the Gentiles. Under the constraint of the witnessing Spirit they bore solemn testimony to the sufferings destined for God's Christ, and to the certain glories to which they would lead. They tried by search and investigation to discover more concerning the date and the character of the times thus indicated. It was revealed to them that their ministry would most directly profit not their own age but those for whom the foretold grace was intended. It is these very things which, now that the time of their fulfilment has come, have been announced by preachers of the gospel, who have been empowered to do so by the same Holy Spirit, especially sent from heaven in order to equip them to bear witness. The wonder, which ought to call forth worship and thanksgiving to God, not only from Peter's readers but also from all who live in this day of salvation, is that we should be the favoured people to share in the benefit of that amazing manifestation of God's grace, which others in the universe, such as prophets and angels, yearn so much to know more about.

The prophets . . . who prophesied of the grace that should come unto you refers to the utterances of those who predicted that God's undeserved, saving mercy would be extended to Gentiles. There are many passages of this kind in the Old Testament. For an apostolic selection see the passages quoted in Rom. ix. 25, 26, 33, x. 11, 13, 20, xv. 9–12, 21. The word *charis, grace,* is used, particularly in the Acts and by Paul, in connection with this extension of salvation to the Gentiles. Paul also uses the word with reference to his own commission to preach to the Gentiles the unsearchable riches of Christ (see Acts xi. 23, xv. 11; Eph. iii. 2, 8). 'The surprising mercy of God, by which those who had been wholly outside the privileged circle were now the recipients of the Divine favour, seems to have called for a new and impressive name which might be the watchword of the larger dispensation.'[1] Christ had Himself foretold and commanded this development, so unexpected by His first Jewish disciples (see Mk. xiii. 10; Mt. xxviii. 19).

The prophets also testified that before such 'glories' (RV) could be realized God's Christ must suffer (see, for example, Is. lii. 14, 15). There is here parallel phraseology, suggesting

[1] J. Armitage Robinson, *Commentary on Ephesians,* 1922, 2nd edition, p. 224.

connection and yet obvious contrast between 'the grace' that was destined to come 'unto you' Gentiles, and 'the sufferings' that were destined to happen 'unto Christ' (see RV mg.). The preposition *eis*, 'unto', occurs in both phrases. The prophets thus testified to three things: first, that God's Christ must suffer; second, that this was for Him the way of entrance into His glory (cf. Lk. xxiv. 25–27), the unusual plural 'glories' stressing the manifold consequences; third, that outstanding among the results of this suffering would be the extension of saving grace to Gentile outsiders. Such developments—that God's Christ should suffer, and that Gentiles should be saved— were both unexpected by the Jews, the first wholly, the second largely, in spite of the explicit prophecies and promises of the Old Testament Scriptures.

What made the prophets thus testify was *the Spirit of Christ which was in them*. Indeed, it was His witness rather than theirs. The surprising content of the witness thus given made the human utterers of it eager to discover more concerning its full meaning, and particularly concerning the time and manner of its fulfilment. Such a statement implies unmistakably that what they prophesied was not of their own imagining or devising, but that they were carried out of themselves and gave utterance to testimony, which came not from themselves but from God (cf. Jn. xi. 49–52; 2 Pet. i. 19–21).

In answer to their quest for fuller understanding these prophets were made aware that they were ministering not to themselves but to those who were to live in the coming day of fulfilment. Such a testimony confirms Paul's repeated state- ment (see Rom. xv. 4; 1 Cor. x. 11) that the Old Testament Scriptures were meant in the purpose of God primarily to provide instruction for Christian believers. So we Christians can find in them God-given help to appreciate the grace of God. They 'are able to make (us) wise unto salvation through faith which is in Christ Jesus' (2 Tim. iii. 15). We do well, therefore, not to let the so-called scientific and critical approach rob us of the distinctive and divinely-intended Christian use of the Old Testament.

The activity of God's Spirit among men is doubly connected with God's Christ. God's gift of the Spirit to men is fundamentally God's gift to His Christ. Jesus became 'the Christ' when He was thus uniquely 'anointed' with the Spirit. All other men, who share in an experience of the Spirit's anointing, share in the anointing given to the incarnate Son of God, i.e. in *the Spirit of Christ*. Also, the primary concern of the activity of the Spirit, as thus given to others, is to glorify Christ, to bear witness to Him, to take of the things of Jesus and to show them unto men (see Jn. xv. 26, xvi. 14). This is what the Spirit did in Old Testament times through the prophets; He testified beforehand of Christ (cf. Rev. xix. 10). At Pentecost there was a special, fresh sending of the same Spirit from heaven by the exalted Christ, for the same purpose, i.e. to ensure that the good news about Jesus as the Christ is preached to the ends of the earth (see Acts i. 8, v. 30–32). So there is a Spirit-inspired unity in the testimony of Old Testament prophets and New Testament apostles or gospel missionaries. It is through their combined witness that men embrace God's saving grace in Christ, and His Church is built (see Eph. ii. 18–22).

The verb *parakuptein* translated *to look into* means 'to stoop or bend down to look'. It is also used in Lk. xxiv. 12; Jn. xx. 5, 11; Jas. i. 25. Thus do heavenly beings, such as angels, take an intense, wondering interest in what God is doing here on earth for the salvation of men (cf. Lk. xv. 10; Eph. iii. 10).

III. THE CHALLENGE TO LIVE DIFFERENTLY
(i. 13–ii. 3)

Because of the salvation, which they are called to enjoy, believers in Christ are here confronted with a demand for transformed conduct. Compelling appeal is made to their divine calling and their new relation to God as Father, to the character of God Himself as holy and as Judge of all men, to Christ's redeeming work and resurrection glory, and to their own experience of new birth through response to the truth. The need is stressed for an active response of mind, and for a proper discipline of behaviour. There is explicit exhortation to forsake evil in thought, word and deed, to become holy, to let life be governed by active reverence for God, to love one another, and to feed on appropriate spiritual food. This food is the Word of God which, because it shares in the vitality and durability of its divine author, is the dynamic force which God uses to bring all these changes about, first to cleanse and to quicken, and then to promote growth to full salvation. All should have an eager appetite for it who have once tasted how kind the Lord is.

a. God's purpose for His elect (i. 13–16)

God's purpose for those whom He calls is twofold: first, that they may do His will, or practise obedience, and second, that they may become like Him, or grow in holiness. In contrast to this, men's lives before conversion to God are lived in ignorance of Him and of His will. They are consequently dominated by the satisfaction of their own desires and the copying of the prevailing fashions of this world, instead of by devotion to the doing of God's commandments and the imitation of God's character. Therefore, when men respond to the call of God in the gospel, a radical change must be made. They must cease to live according to the old fashion, and must seek instead to reproduce the divine family likeness of holiness in all their behaviour. This is but to implement the pattern of God's intention for His people as indicated plainly in the ancient, God-given law.

13. *Wherefore* indicates that the exhortations which follow are grounded upon the preceding statements. It is typical of the way in which the Epistles always base ethical demands on doctrinal exposition. This logical sequence is also marked by a noteworthy change of emphasis. Salvation, we have been explicitly and repeatedly told, is embraced and enjoyed by faith. We have to receive it, acknowledging our complete dependence upon God and His saving grace. But, once this response has been begun, we are emphatically challenged to realize that energetic disciplined activity is now rightly expected of us, and that we shall properly fulfil our new obligations and exercise our new privileges only if we make it. Since we now enjoy a new relation to God, a new liberty in Christ, and a new life in the Spirit, it is up to us to give them active expression in obedience to God's will.

Gird up the loins of your mind is a metaphor suited to men of the Middle East, who wore long gowns which were 'girded up' when energetic effort was contemplated. The equivalent in our world is obviously to 'roll up one's sleeves' or to 'take off one's coat to it'. We must begin to act as those who mean business. Note that it is in the realm of the *mind* that this serious new activity is demanded. Conversion to Christ and regeneration by the Spirit are meant to be accompanied by mental awakening, by a new exercise of powers of understanding now divinely released and renewed (cf. Rom. xii. 2; Eph. iv. 17, 18, 23).

The word *nēphontes, be sober*, refers primarily to abstinence from wine; used metaphorically it describes moral alertness or sobriety generally, for example, in speech and conduct. Here it describes a life of disciplined self-control in contrast to the reckless irresponsibility of self-indulgence on the one hand, and of religious ecstasy on the other. According to the New Testament the Spirit-filled man is not carried away into abnormal extravagance of behaviour like someone drunk, but acts as a man in full possession of himself (see Gal. v. 22, 23, RV mg.).

The adverb *teleiōs*, translated *to the end*, means 'completely' or 'without reserve'. Such sure and radiant expectation should be an unfailing mark of the believer in Christ. For he has an adequate ground for such hopefulness in the kindness conferred on him through Christ's appearing. The last phrase of verse 13 indicates not what to expect, but why it is always possible to be hopeful. Believers in Christ can be sure of His favour when He appears. The use of the present participle in the Greek, meaning 'is being brought', in conjunction with the word *grace*, may mean that Christ's first advent is in mind (cf. Tit. ii. 11).

The present continuous tense of the participle suggests that, whenever Christ is revealed to the believer, past, present or future, it is to confer benefit.

14, 15. *As obedient children* may express what the phrase implies in the context, but the RV rendering 'children of obedience' more exactly represents the Greek and the expression is best understood as a Hebraism, describing not children of God who are obedient but those whose 'mother' is obedience, i.e. those whose prevailing spirit is obedience, and who are given up to its habitual practice or expression (cf. the phrase 'children of disobedience' in Eph. ii. 2, v. 6, or 'children of transgression' in Is. lvii. 4). As verse 2 has indicated, such obedience to God on their part of the elect is the divinely pre-determined goal of their calling—what Paul calls the 'obedience of faith' (see Rom. i. 5, xvi. 26, cf. vi. 13–18)—and the proper expression of their God-given new life. Such activity, therefore, ought to be characteristic of them, and can rightly be demanded from them.

Not fashioning yourselves according to . . . but as he . . . is holy, so be ye holy. Full response to the challenge of the call of God in the gospel inevitably has two sides. It involves no longer doing what we always have done, and also becoming something which hitherto we have not been. This must be seen in every detail of our dealings with other people. Exhortations of this twofold kind were obviously characteristic of the instructions given to converts in New Testament times (cf. Eph. iv. 17–24; Tit. ii. 11–14), and may well have been based on, and inspired by, similar instructions in the Old Testament law of holiness (see Lv. xviii. 1–5, 24–30).

The Greek verb for 'to fashion' denotes something superficial, transient, changeable. The same word occurs in Rom. xii. 2, 'Be not fashioned according to this world' (RV) (cf. 1 Cor. vii. 31). This old way of living, which is now to be given up, is further described as senseless indulgence, as a gratification of, and domination by, natural appetites, which run to evil and harmful excess because not governed by any true knowledge and consequent standard. The *ignorance* is primarily ignorance of God, especially as He is now known in Christ, and refers either particularly to heathen godlessness (see 1 Thes. iv. 5), or more generally to the spiritual blindness of the unconverted, whether Jew or Gentile (see 1 Tim. i. 13). For *as he which hath called you is holy* the RV mg. reads 'like the Holy One which called you'. The Greek adjective *hagios* may here be a virtual noun. There are places in the Old Testament where the corresponding Hebrew adjective is used in the sense of 'the Holy One' to identify God Himself (see Is. xl. 25, xli. 14, 16, 20). The new standard of living for the Christian, the true model to be copied, is thus nothing less than God Himself. It is our new personal relation to Him in consequence of His call that precedes and provides the ground for this new moral demand. We are now to be 'imitators of God, as beloved children' (Eph. v. 1, RV), to be perfect as our heavenly Father is perfect (Mt. v. 48), to reproduce the family likeness. This is the pattern and the goal of our calling (cf. Col. iii. 10), and is to be given full practical outworking in all our behaviour.

There are other significant references in this Epistle to God's call and its consequences (see ii. 9, 20, 21, v. 10). The exhortation *genēthēte, be ye*, means 'become' or 'show yourselves to be'. The word *anastrophē*, translated *conversation* (in its old English sense), is not limited in reference to 'speech', but covers 'conduct' as a whole. Its embrace here is made more complete by the added adjective meaning 'every form of'.

16. The RV 'ye shall be' correctly renders the Greek, but the AV wording rightly expresses its virtual imperative force. Appeal is here made to the Old Testament revelation and its significant authoritative disclosure of God's purpose. When He called the Israelites out of Egypt, He did so in order to become their God in a new and special way. He then demanded that those, who were thus to become His people, should be holy like Himself (see Ex. vi. 6, 7, xix. 3–6; Lv. xi. 45, xix. 2, xx. 7, 26; cf. 1 Thes. iv. 7). So the first and sufficient reason why God's people should keep themselves from uncleanness is because the

Lord their God is holy; only so can they respond to their calling and enjoy intimate fellowship with Him. It is, therefore, the revelation of God's character and the call to be intimately related to Him that make holiness an obligation. Religion and ethics are thus in the biblical revelation fundamentally welded together. True devotion to God must find expression in holy living. Ethical conduct finds its standard and pattern in the character of God Himself. Also, this governing principle of conformity to the character of God as the goal of true morality is so explicitly and authoritatively enshrined in the God-given law of the Old Testament that a Christian apostle appeals to it as decisive—*because it is written.* Such an appeal bears witness to the divine origin, supreme authority and abiding truth of the Mosaic revelation. The New Testament gospel does not leave it behind, but confronts us afresh with the obligation, and the new Christian urge and power, to fulfil it.

b. A call to the redeemed to fear God (i. 17–21)

In further amplification of the challenge to live differently, these verses emphasize the spirit of reverence or awe in which Christians, aware of being temporary sojourners only, ought to live their earthly lives. They should be moved to such attitudes by the knowledge that, like the Israelites who were brought out of Egypt to know God as their God in a new way, so they, too, have been redeemed from the bondage of empty conventional living to know and call upon God as Father in all the intimacy of a new relationship. Surely it should fill them with awe to know themselves thus related to the Judge of all the earth? Also, just as in Egypt the Israelites were shielded from judgment by the shed blood of the Passover lamb, so Christians have been saved from actually knowing God as their Judge through the precious blood of Christ. This amazing sacrifice for their redemption God Himself fore-ordained before the world was made. Christ has fulfilled it for their benefit. God has shown His acceptance of Christ, and of His death for sinners deserving judgment, by exalting Him in resurrection to glory. So through Christ they can look to God in sure confidence and hope, and see in the glory thus given to the exalted Jesus the promise and pattern of their own full salvation—the promised land or inheritance into which they are to be brought after earth's pilgrimage is over (remember verses 3–5). Such awareness ought to make all who share in it face life here in a new way. There should be a sense of awe before God, and an awareness that they are only sojourners here.

17. The RV 'if ye call on him as Father' rightly expresses the meaning of the Greek. The same verb *epikaleisthai* followed by an accusative occurs in Acts xxv. 11, 'I appeal unto Caesar' (see also Acts vii. 59, RV). Christians are now privileged to 'invoke', or to appeal for aid to, God as Father. There may well be an implied reference here to the way Jesus Himself taught His disciples to pray, saying, 'Father' (Lk. xi. 2, RV; cf. Rom. viii. 15; Gal. iv. 6). Here 'Father' is made very emphatic in Greek by being put before the verb. This emphasizes the wonder that Christians are able to invoke the supreme impartial Judge by such a name. Also, according to the Old Testament law of holiness, reverence was first to be given in society to parents even more than to the judge (see, for example, Lv. xix. 2, 3). How much more should such reverence be supremely given to God, thus known not as Judge but as Father? Yet, on the other hand, just as the fact that God is holy puts upon His people the obligation themselves to become holy, so the truth that they are now related, as children to a Father, should make them spend their lives with a new concern, and under a new constraint, namely, to win from Him praise rather than punishment (cf. Dt. x. 12–20; 2 Cor. v. 10, 11). He unfailingly (*judgeth* translates a present participle 'judging') and impartially deals with men in judgment according to the actual work of each particular individual. The adverb translated *without respect of persons* means without undue regard to mere superficial appearance, i.e. as distinct from inherent character. *In fear* means in that kind of healthy and holy reverence for God, which is the condition of all true understanding of life, and which itself constrains men to delight in God's ways and to depart from evil (see Ps. cxi. 10, RV, cxii. 1; Pr. xvi. 6; Is. xi. 2–4; Lk. xii. 4, 5; and Peter's words in Acts x. 34, 35).

The time of your sojourning here. The word *here* is not in the Greek, but its addition rightly indicates the reference of the phrase to the life of Christians in this world, where their residence should consciously be not settled and permanent, but 'alongside' and 'in passing' only. The preposition *para* with which the word *paroikia, sojourning,* begins conveys this force, in contrast to *kata* ('down'), in the word for settled abode, *katoikia* (Acts xvii. 26). *Paroikia* is used in Acts xiii. 17 of the Israelites' 'sojourn' in Egypt. So Christians are to live in this world as in a place to which they do not belong, and where they do not expect for ever to stay. This is the original and scriptural idea of a *parochial* outlook—in radical contrast to the acquired meaning of this English derivative from *paroikia.*

18, 19. Christians need to remember that, like the Israelites whom God brought out of Egypt, they have been rescued from bondage; bondage in their case to a way of life that was *vain* or empty. It lacked reverence for the true God and, in consequence, it lacked a proper regard for real values. It produced no worthwhile result. It was wholly determined by inherited usage, by tradition and convention. From this they were *redeemed.* Here not only is the idea of redemption introduced, but there is also actual mention of the ransom price. This corresponds to our Lord's own declaration of the purpose of His mission—'to give his life a ransom for many' (Mk. x. 45). What needs explicit recognition is the outstanding character of this price. For it is not anything connected with this transient, corruptible world, such as silver or gold, but the infinitely *precious* or 'highly valued' *blood of Christ,* who, like a flawless and spotless *lamb,* was offered in sacrifice.

Blood here signifies, as commonly in such contexts, blood shed, or life laid down, in sacrificial death. *Without blemish and*

without spot corresponds to the ritual requirement of the
Passover and other offerings (see Ex. xii. 5; Lv. xxii. 19, 20;
Dt. xv. 21). The lamb to be sacrificed had to be without either
inherent flaw or external defilement. Applied to a person these
phrases signify moral integrity and perfection. They describe
one not liable to die for his own sin, and so possessing a life
which could be offered to atone for others' sin. It is significant
that Jesus and His death are here interpreted in terms fully
understandable only by those who know the Old Testament
Scriptures. Jesus is to be recognized as fulfilling the office of
Messiah; and His death is to be regarded as sacrificial and
substitutionary, and so redemptive—the death of the sinless
for the benefit and release of the sin-bound. It is this recognition of what redemption has cost, which puts those who share
in it under added obligation to order their lives in a corres-
pondingly worthy manner.

20. In the words *foreordained* (RV 'foreknown') *before the
foundation of the world* the Person and work of God's Christ are
declared to have had a place in the eternal counsel of God, a
place in God's mind and purpose before the created order was
established. We are thus made aware that man's fall into sin
and consequent bondage did not take God by surprise. He had
foreseen it; and He had ready His remedy for it, and His way
of redemption from it. He knew beforehand what He would do
when the need for it emerged. What He knew, first of all, was
the Person by whom He would do it, namely, His own Son,
functioning in this specially ordained capacity as God's
'Christ', so called because anointed and equipped for His task
by God's Spirit, and fulfilling His appointed task by becoming
in redemptive sacrifice the true Passover lamb. So, not only
the idea of a coming Messiah, but also the idea of a Messiah
who should die to redeem His people, alike formed part of
God's preconceived plan for this world before its creation (cf.
Eph. i. 4–10).

But was manifest in these last times for you (better, as in RV, 'at
the end of the times for your sake'). The Christian dispensation,

the point and period in history of Christ's coming, is here regarded as the climax and consummation of the previous ages (cf. Heb. i. 1, 2, ix. 26). The word translated *was manifest* (*phaneroō* in the passive) is similarly used of the incarnation, particularly with reference to Christ's sacrificial death, in Heb. ix. 26 and 1 Jn. iii. 5. This divine counsel of eternity, thus fulfilled by the divine manifestation in history, was specially directed towards the salvation of those who, like Peter's readers, were otherwise to be reckoned as sinners and complete Gentile outsiders.

21. The repeated phrase *in God* translates *eis Theon*. This wording suggests active approach and committal, believing 'into God'. In two ways God has acted decisively to assure us that we may thus come to God and put our faith in Him. First, as we have just seen, there is what Christ has done (in the fulfilment of His messianic office) to redeem us, or, as Peter puts it in iii. 18, to 'bring us to God'. Second, there is what God Himself has done to demonstrate both His acceptance of Christ's Person and work (by raising Him from the dead), and His pleasure to reward Him as Man for the benefit of His people (by giving Him the full bodily and heavenly glory destined for humanity). Those for whom Christ died have, therefore, double ground for coming to God. They may approach in confidence, counting on God to receive them, and in hope, expecting that in the end they, too, are to share the same glory which Christ already enjoys (cf. Rom. v. 2, viii. 16–21). Note how explicit is the indication that salvation in Christ is in its fulfilment divine both in origin and in goal, an act of God to bring men to Himself.

c. Expressing the new life (i. 22–ii. 3)

The challenge to live differently is renewed. The ground of appeal is once again the twofold change which response to the gospel has brought into their lives. They have found cleansing; and so they should be putting off sinful habits. They have been given new life from God; and so they should be expressing it in corresponding new activity. The particular new activity to which they are here exhorted is brotherly love. This is complemented by an exhortation to put off all attitudes and actions towards others which are a denial of such brotherly love, and must prevent its positive expression. Also, they are reminded that they owe their experience of cleansing, and their entrance into new life, to the Word of God, which they have heard preached in the gospel of truth to which they have responded. They are, therefore, exhorted to further the full growth of this new life by eagerly seeking for it the same sort of nourishment (i.e. through the Word) from the Lord, whose kindness they have already tasted.

22, 23a. *Obeying the truth* obviously refers to their response to the gospel. The phrase distinguishes Christianity from the errors of heathen religions as *the truth* and emphasizes that response involves not mere detached assent but active submission (cf. i. 2, 14). Such true response issues on the one hand in cleansing and on the other in quickening or new birth. These are the characteristic initial blessings of the gospel, otherwise described as forgiveness of sins and the gift of the Spirit (see, for example, Acts ii. 38). These two benefits and the believer's personal entrance into their enjoyment are both clearly symbolized in and by Christian baptism, which some think is, therefore, implied here. This view is supported by the fact that the participles translated *purified* and *born again* are both in the perfect tense, referring to one decisive act in the past with abiding consequences. Over against such a suggestion it is important to notice that the text itself here makes no explicit reference at all to baptism, but it does make a reiterated explicit reference to *the truth* or *word of God*, which is the instrument which God uses to effect cleansing and quickening (cf. our Lord's own statements in Jn. xv. 3, xvii. 17, vi. 63b). (What the sacrament of baptism does is to confirm and illustrate the truth and efficacy of the Word to the individual, who in response to it counts on, and confesses his faith in, the Lord; cf. iii. 21.)

Unto unfeigned love of the brethren. God's quickening work gives us both a new nature to express, and new relatives—brethren in Christ—towards whom to express it. Christians ought to love one another, not as if they were brethren, but because they are brethren. Such love should, therefore, be *unfeigned*, not pretended or put on in superficial 'play-acting' or in wordy, sentimental profession. Rather it should genuinely come 'from the heart' (rv); and it should be engaged in *fervently*. The Greek word *ektenōs* does not mean 'with warmth', but rather 'with full intensity', literally 'at full stretch' or in an 'all out' manner (cf. iv. 8; see also ii. 17, iii. 8).

23b-25. The new life from God is 'begotten' (rv) of incorruptible divine seed. Those who possess it become 'partakers of the divine nature' (2 Pet. i. 4). This new life is communicated to men, or men are made to possess it, through the divine word—the word which had been actively brought unto Peter's readers in dynamic ministry (cf. 'The seed is the word of God'; Lk. viii. 11). This seed or word of God shares in the character of its author. It is *not . . . corruptible . . . but . . . incorruptible . . . which liveth and abideth.* In the Greek these last two words *liveth* and *abideth* may grammatically be taken with 'God' (cf. Dn. vi. 26); but as in the following Old Testament quotation and in the comment in verse 25 the reference is explicitly to God's utterance, it seems preferable to regard that as the reference throughout (cf. Heb. iv. 12, rv).

What Peter asserts, therefore, with a quotation from Is. xl. 6–8 to enforce it, is that God's *word* lives and abides. It never becomes obsolete or a dead letter. It continues to speak to men unchanging, vital, present truth. It continues to find completion and vindication in unfailing fulfilment. For God, by His Spirit, is continually confirming its authority to men as His abiding word, and demonstrating its worth as a living word by fulfilling its promises in outworked deeds (cf. Is. lv. 10, 11).

In Is. xl. 6–8 the transitoriness of the natural creation is contrasted with the unfailing continuance of the divine utterance. Human beings without exception (i.e. *all flesh*) are like the grass of the field; human *glory* is like the flowers, i.e. the glory of natural vegetation. For all alike have their brief day and then become, as men say, 'dead and gone', the exact opposite of 'living and abiding'. So, in a created order which is bound to pass away, it is God's word which offers men a confidence which is more secure and participation in life which is more abiding (cf. Mk. xiii. 31). No wonder its proclamation to heathen outsiders is described as an 'evangelization' or heralding of good tidings.

ii. 1. The new divinely-enabled and divinely-intended life of love, consequent upon being born into God's family as His children, cannot be lived unless attitudes and activities towards our brethren which contradict and frustrate it, are decisively renounced. Explicit exhortation is therefore given to put away every form of such anti-social evil, particularly those forms in which it commonly first begins to find expression, i.e. in heart attitude and motive, in casual utterance, and in unreal and unworthy participation in outward fellowship.

Kakia, malice (RV 'wickedness'), is possibly best understood in a general sense (cf. Jas. i. 21, 'naughtiness'), i.e. all kinds of evil conduct. In New Testament usage, however, the word often has more particular reference to active ill-will, 'the vicious nature which is bent on doing harm to others' (J. B. Lightfoot). Similarly, in active wrong relations with their brethren individuals become skilful in every form of *guile* or 'deceit'; and prone to engage in acts of hypocrisy, in which, like Ananias and Sapphira (Acts v. 1–11), they outwardly play a part which appears acceptable, but inwardly they are insincerely serving the interests of their own reputation or material advantage.

Another frequent cause of disharmony and virtual strife, particularly in a fellowship such as a Christian congregation in which participation is completely voluntary, is *envy*. This attitude often finds expression in *evil speaking*, in running down the individual of whom one is jealous, possibly because he has been given a position and ministry for which one fancied oneself. As with *hypocrisies* above, since the nouns are both in the plural the sense is 'acts of envy and of evil speaking'.

2. The Christian's new God-given life needs appropriate nourishment, if it is to grow into the full enjoyment and realization of salvation. This nourishment should, therefore, be sought after and delighted in with the same intense zest and active eagerness with which very young infants yearn for and welcome feeding-time. The nourishment thus to be longed for is described as *to logikon adolon gala, the sincere milk of the word,* or as RV renders it, 'the spiritual milk which is without guile'. The adjective *logikon* means 'reasonable' or 'rational' (cf. Rom. xii. 1). Here it may suggest that the milk in view is food for the mind rather than for the stomach. If the idea in milk 'consisting of word' rather than 'of liquid', there is probably some intended connection in thought with the previous reference to the divine *logos* or 'word' (i. 23) as the instrument used by God to bring about new birth. Just as the proper food for new-born infants is their mothers' milk, so the appropriate nourishment for those 'born again . . . by the word of God' is the *milk of the word.* Note this explicit reference to the word, and the absence of any reference to the sacrament, as the proper means of spiritual nourishment.

The second adjective, *adolon,* means 'guileless', and so 'genuine' or 'pure'. If new-born babes are healthily to grow, their milk should be pure and unadulterated (cf. 2 Cor. iv. 2, where Paul speaks of 'not adulterating (*dolountes*) the word of God'). Also, for the new-born Christian the appropriate 'guileless' food is divinely intended to nourish the guileless life. The word 'guileless' is here in direct contrast to *all guile* (verse 1), which Peter exhorts his readers to put away. Taken together these two verses suggest that wrong relations with our fellow-Christians may put us off our food. Only those Christians who cut out unworthy attitudes and activities towards their brethren, can have a proper, healthy appetite for their necessary spiritual food. And only those who thus take such food will grow to Christian maturity and so experience full salvation. As in RV 'unto salvation' should follow *grow thereby*.

3. The phraseology here obviously follows that of Ps. xxxiv. 8. The opening word *ei*, *if*, introduces a reason rather than a query. The sense is 'since' or 'seeing that'. RSV renders, 'For you have tasted the kindness of the Lord'. This indicates both whence the Christian draws his life and nourishment, i.e. from the Lord Himself through His word, and also what should have given him this intense and eager appetite for more, namely, vital personal experience of the loving-kindness of the Lord. So the God-given word is to be desired not for its own sake, but because it enables us to feed upon its author, and to appropriate His grace.

IV. THE PRIVILEGES OF BELONGING TO THE PEOPLE OF GOD (ii. 4-10)

All who come to Christ in response to this preached word of the gospel find themselves incorporated by their relation to Him into a temple, or rather a priesthood, whose intended function it is through Christ to offer to God acceptable spiritual sacrifices. As was foretold in the Scriptures, Christ is thus divinely appointed to be the unifying centre of a building of God. The privilege of a place in it is promised to all who believe in Christ. On the other hand, there are those who refuse to acknowledge Him, and who reject the word that promises benefit to those who believe in Him. In this way the same Christ becomes to them an occasion of disobedience and consequent judgment. But all who acknowledge Him find themselves members of God's elect people. Their transference from the outer darkness into the full light of enjoying the divine mercy, and belonging to His specially chosen people, is itself an exhibition to the universe of God's virtuous doings.

a. The new 'spiritual house' (ii. 4, 5)

Here is another description, first of the way in which men

become Christians, and second of the consequence of their doing so. Men become Christians simply by coming to Christ, here called *a living stone*. Those who thus come, themselves become *as lively* (RV 'living') *stones*, and are integrated together to form *a spiritual house*. Because these constituent stones are 'living', i.e. themselves people, they thus form not only a temple, in which God is to be worshipped, but also *an holy priesthood*, or company of consecrated ministers, who offer the worship. As Christian priests their distinctive calling is *to offer up . . . sacrifices*, which are *acceptable to God* because they are *spiritual* in character, and because they are offered *by* (RV 'through') *Jesus Christ*, and in virtue of the worshipper's living union with Him.

4. The compound verb *proserchesthai*, together with the repeated preposition *pros*, *to whom* or 'towards whom', expresses the idea of drawing near with intention both to stay and to enjoy personal fellowship. The word is used in the LXX of drawing near to God in worship, to offer prayer and sacrifice. The connected word 'proselyte', i.e. one who has drawn near, was used to describe a Gentile convert to Judaism, an outsider who had become a member of God's people. So here the thought is that *ye also* (*kai autoi*, verse 5), i.e. even those who had been complete outsiders, 'which in time past were not a people' (verse 10) can, simply by coming to Christ, find entrance into membership and full, active privilege in the people of God (cf. Eph. ii. 11–22).

Verse 4 is clearly a reference to Christ in language derived, as Peter explicitly indicates in verses 6–8, from the Old Testament Scriptures. It is equally clearly a reference to the central facts of the gospel, the crucifixion, resurrection, and heavenly exaltation of Christ. This *stone* is *living*, not only because He is a Person, but also because He has been 'raised from the dead' and 'dieth no more' (Rom. vi. 9), and is Himself 'a life-giving spirit' (1 Cor. xv. 45, RV). He has been *disallowed* or 'rejected' (RV), i.e. disapproved and refused as unsuitable by men. This refers particularly to the rejection of His claim to be the

Messiah by the responsible Jewish religious leaders. The same word describing disapproval occurs in our Lord's predictions of His rejection by the elders, chief priests and scribes (see Mk. viii. 31; Lk. ix. 22). By contrast He is 'with God elect, precious' (RV). This statement is set in direct opposition to the statement of human rejection. God contradicted men's verdict, and declared His acceptance of Jesus as the Christ, by exalting Him. This was the central emphasis of the gospel, which Peter preached (see Acts ii. 23, 24, 32, 33, iv. 11, 12, v. 30, 31, x. 39, 40). The phrase *ho eklektos*, the *chosen of God*, was a description of God's Christ (see Lk. xxiii. 35). In thus exalting Him God expressed His attitude to Him, and marked Him out before all, as one uniquely selected and *precious* (RV mg. 'honourable'). While the Hebrew underlying this word in Is. xxviii. 16 means 'costly', here the Greek *entimos* means rather 'honoured' or 'prized', and so 'highly esteemed' (see Lk. vii. 2, 'dear'; Phil. ii. 29, 'in reputation'; Lk. xiv. 8, 'honourable').

5. Talking metaphorically those who acknowledge Christ as the exalted stone themselves become, by reason of their relation to Him, *as lively* (RV 'living') *stones* to be built into God's house. Here Peter is expounding truth to which his Christian name 'Peter' (i.e. 'a stone') testified, and truth which he had learnt from the Lord Himself. It was when Simon similarly acknowledged Jesus as God's Christ, that Jesus in effect had said to him: 'Now you are a stone; and I want many similar stones, because I intend with them to build a Church; and to build it upon, or in relation to, Myself, thus confessed as Christ, as the basic Rock or unifying chief cornerstone' (see Mt. xvi. 15–18). Note that the phrase *ye . . . are built up* implies that men enter the Church by coming to Christ, not that they become joined to Christ by entering the Church.

A spiritual house. The following references to priesthood and to the offering of sacrifice show that the kind of house in view is a shrine or temple (cf. Ps. lxix. 9; Jn. ii. 17; Is. lvi. 7; Mk. xi. 17). Thus, in the Christian and spiritual fulfilment of the earthly figures of true religion, God's chosen sanctuary is His people. In contrast to Judaism, in which only a selected number from a single tribe functioned as priests, in this new Christian community all enter the *priesthood* and can, therefore, themselves constitute the sanctuary, in whose midst God's presence is manifested, and by whom worship is offered to God. What was unthinkable in Judaism is fundamental to Christianity; proselytes become priests. The priesthood and its ministry are a status and a privilege enjoyed by the whole laity, by every member of the people of God. They are no longer restricted to a specially qualified minority, on whose ministries the majority of the people is dependent.

The characteristic and distinctive activity of priests is *to offer up spiritual sacrifices* The ones now to be offered are no longer animal and ceremonial, but spiritual and moral. Even in the Old Testament contrition, prayer, praise and thanksgiving are all described as acts of sacrifice (see Pss. l. 14, li. 17, cvii. 22, cxli. 2). Clearly here, especially in view of the added qualification 'spiritual', the kind of sacrifices meant are the daily devotion of the life in obedience (cf. Rom. xii. 1), praise and thanksgiving to God (Heb. xiii. 15), and practical ministry to the needs of men (Heb. xiii. 16).

When religion was a matter of ceremonial animal sacrifice, it was a question of great moment whether the sacrifice would prove acceptable, which by its very nature such sacrifice could never properly be (see Heb. x. 1–10). Christians are assured that their sacrifices will be *acceptable to God*, both because what is pleasing to God is the spiritual worship of willing, rational and moral obedience, or freely-chosen personal devotion, such as animals could not render, and because those now joined to Christ are sure of acceptance when they offer their sacrifices through Him. The phrase *by* (RV 'through') *Jesus Christ* may be connected either with the verb 'to offer up' or with the word 'acceptable'.

b. The chief corner-stone (ii. 6–8)

Peter quotes the prophetic Scriptures to show first that Christ's unique position as the chief corner-stone of the new building was foreseen and foreordained of God, and then that both the profit to be gained by all those who believe in Him, and the fact that to the unresponsive who disobey the word the same Christ is like the one desirable stone which foolish builders have thrown out, or like a stone which causes some to trip over it, have also been clearly foretold. The same stone that by divine appointment is the satisfying confidence of the believing brings down the unbelieving in inevitable judgment (cf. Mt. xxi. 42, 44). In the original the same verb, *tithēmi*, is used in the present active in verse 6, *I lay* (i.e. 'set' or 'place'), and in the aorist passive in verse 8, *were appointed*.

Three important passages from the Old Testament (Is. xxviii. 16; Ps. cxviii. 22; Is. viii. 14), which all use the same 'stone' metaphor, are combined to express the full truth. There is some ancient Jewish evidence to suggest that 'the stone' was regarded by Jews as a title for the Messiah. It is obviously with this full personal application to Christ that these Scriptures are here quoted.

It is particularly noteworthy how much of the pattern of Peter's gospel about Christ can here be seen to be metaphorically suggested. As the one who claimed to be the Messiah, Jesus was rejected by the very builders whom one would have expected to welcome Him with acclamation. They found in Him One who completely offended them. Yet He is the One whom God has set in place as the chief corner-stone of the new house of God. All who believe in Him, thus exalted, are not only not disappointed; they are not only joined as stones to the one great central unifying stone; they also share His acceptance and place of honour in God's sight.

Such Scriptures were obviously in general use in the early Church to explain both the surprising Jewish rejection of Christ and the essential character of the new people of God as a 'spiritual house' to be built up by inviting complete outsiders simply to believe in the exalted Lord (cf. Acts iv. 10–12; Rom. ix. 32, 33, x. 8–13).

6. The sense of *dioti*, *Wherefore*, is better expressed by 'Because' (RV) or 'For' (RSV). The same word is so rendered in i. 16 and 24. Note that in each case it is used to introduce, and to appeal to, a relevant and decisive quotation from the Old Testament. The word *graphē*, *scripture*, is in the singular, and has no article (see RV 'in scripture'). It is therefore not a reference to the Scriptures (plural) in general, nor to the particular passage here quoted; rather it is a way of saying, 'it stands written' (cf. i. 16, 'it is written'). The Scriptures which are thus introduced are treated as fulfilled in Christ's heavenly exaltation. He is the *chief corner stone . . . the head of the corner*. Since Christ is therefore at the top, rather than at the bottom, of the new building (given from the throne to be 'the head over all things to the church', as Paul puts it in Eph. i. 22), the thought of Him as the 'chief corner stone' rather than the foundation stone is particularly apt. It is to Christ thus on the throne that men must come; it is Jesus thus exalted as Lord whom men must acknowledge in order to be joined to His saved community. The *Sion* in which this fulfilment takes place is the heavenly Jerusalem (cf. Ps. cx. 1, 2; Heb. iv. 14, 16, xii. 22–24).

7. Peter proceeds to stress both by scriptural quotations and by his own testimony that the simple, single and sufficient condition of realized benefit is faith only—faith in Christ. This benefit he describes (see RV and RV mg.) as a share in Christ's 'preciousness' or 'honour'; in other words the exaltation to the throne given to Christ by God is also given to those who *believe* in Him to share, or to derive benefit from (cf. Eph. ii. 5, 6; Heb. vii. 25).

The Greek participle behind the word *disobedient* means 'disbelieving' rather than 'disobeying'. Without the article it refers to the general type; it does not identify any particular individuals. So RV renders 'but for such as disbelieve'. *The stone which the builders disallowed*; better, as in RV, 'rejected'. Stones were examined and approved before they were used in first-class building. Rejected stones were described, and perhaps in some way marked, as 'disapproved' (cf. Paul's reference to becoming a 'castaway' or 'throw out'; 1 Cor. ix. 27).

8. The idea behind the words *a stone of stumbling* . . . is that of a stone or rock which lies in the road so that travellers knock against it or get tripped up by it. It is thus that Christ, once He is revealed, inescapably stands in the way of those who refuse to respond to the testimony about Him. *The word*, both spoken and living, becomes a stumbling-block to those who are *disobedient*, i.e. those who actively revolt against the gospel (see iv. 17). Those who thus disobey are the disbelieving. Unbelief is their root error. Just as true faith manifests itself in obedience, so heart unbelief inevitably finds expression in deliberate disobedience. In this pathway the disobedient, once they thus set themselves against Christ, find that the Christ who had offered to be for them is against them, interrupting their progress. Such outworking of judgment on unbelief is as divinely appointed as the way of salvation through faith in the exalted Christ.

c. The people of God (ii. 9, 10)

These two verses describe, in phraseology all significantly taken from the Old Testament, the kind of company which believers in Christ become. The titles are all corporate, a list of collective nouns, all in the singular.

9. *A chosen generation*, RV 'an elect race', is from Is. xliii. 20. *A royal priesthood* is from Ex. xix. 6. There both the Hebrew and the LXX express the idea of 'a kingdom' as well as a priesthood (cf. Rev. i. 6, v. 10; see RV). Here in 1 Peter the AV expresses well the meaning of the Greek, i.e. a priesthood belonging to, and in the service of, the King. In its only other New Testament occurrence *basileion* is not simply an adjective meaning 'royal' but a virtual noun meaning a 'palace' or 'king's court' (see Lk. vii. 25). It is possible to take it in this sense here, as describing the Christian community as a 'king's house' or 'royal residence'. What, however, seems even more probable (particularly in the light of the distinctive biblical meaning of the Hebrew and Greek words commonly translated 'kingdom', and in the light of statements such as Zc. vi. 13 and Rev. v. 10) is that Christians are here described as sharing with Christ in kingship or sovereignty as well as in priesthood. They are therefore a true hierarchy, called to reign as well as to serve.

An holy nation is from Ex. xix. 6. The Greek *ethnos* is the word commonly used in the plural for the Gentile nations. Israel, as one of the nations, was distinct by reason of being *holy*, i.e. consecrated to God. *A peculiar people*, RV 'a people for (God's) own possession', combines phraseology found in Ex. xix. 5, Is. xliii. 21, and Mal. iii. 17 (cf. Tit. ii. 14; Eph. i. 14, RV). The noun *laos* particularly describes them as the 'laity' or covenant people of God. This is the word elsewhere used of the people of Israel as distinct from the nations (see Acts xxvi. 17, 23; Rom. xv. 10). *That ye should shew forth the praises of him* follows the thought of Is. xliii. 21. *Aretai*, translated *praises* (RV 'excellencies'), means 'virtues', 'eminent qualities', which are not only good in themselves but also rightly secure a reputation for their possessor. The plural suggests not only the essential excellence of God's character, but also the actual deeds by which He revealed it, i.e. by what He has done in bringing outsiders into the enjoyment of such privilege. *Out of darkness into . . . light* is a typical New Testament description of the change which the Christian gospel brought into the lives of converts from heathenism (cf. Acts xxvi. 18; Eph. v. 8; Col. i. 13).

10. The ideas of this verse come from Ho. i. 6–10, ii. 23. Cf. Rom. ix. 23–26, where the reference is explicitly to the calling of a people 'not from the Jews only, but also from the Gentiles' (RV). The perfect participle in the phrase *had not obtained mercy* suggests that as heathen they had long continued in this state. By contrast the aorist participle in the following phrase translated *but now have obtained mercy* points to the decisive occasion of their conversion when, through hearing the gospel, they were brought out of darkness into light.

In the Old Testament such phraseology as is here used indicated God's purpose for the people whom He formed for Himself by redeeming them from bondage in Egypt and later once again openly declared to be His by bringing them back from captivity in Babylon. The use of such phraseology here implies that what is typically and prophetically anticipated in Old Testament history finds its fulfilment in the Christian community. The Church of Christ, so Peter unmistakably asserts, is the true Israel of God, the people of a unique, God-given calling and destiny.

This passage as a whole (ii. 4–10) also indicates that this calling and destiny are fundamentally realized only in and through Christ. He it is who is the 'chosen of God' or God's 'elect'. He is the priest upon His throne who combines in His Person royalty and priesthood. He is given unique privileges as the Holy One of God, and as God's very own Son. These honours He shares, as the Christ, with His people. They are 'for you therefore which believe' (see verse 7, RV and RV mg.). So it is the company of erstwhile outsiders with no status and deserving judgment as sinners who, because of God's mercy towards them in Christ, and because they have come to Him, and believed in Him, are told that they now constitute a community characterized by election, royalty, priesthood, holiness and privileged relation to God as His special people. They are also told that what has thus happened to them, and what they now are by God's doings, is intended to proclaim or advertise to the universe the worthiness of God's works and ways.

V. CHRISTIAN LIVING IN RELATION TO OTHERS (ii. 11–iii. 12)

In a manner typical of the New Testament Epistles Peter now gives both general and particular guidance and exhortation concerning Christian behaviour. This section of the Epistle opens (ii. 11, 12) and ends (iii. 8–12) with exhortations of universal application to all Christians concerning their manner of life in this world, and in relation to their fellow-men. The intervening paragraphs deal in turn with the duties of Christians as citizens, as servants, and as wives and husbands. These exhortations cover the chief human relationships in life, one's relationship, as we might say, to the state, to one's employer, and to one's home and married partner. In introducing Christ's patient submission to undeserved suffering as an example to be imitated, Peter cannot refrain from indicating also the unique atoning character and efficacy of His death (ii. 21–25).

The general emphasis throughout is on active and patient submission, on loyal and disciplined devotion, freely rendered, constrained by reverence for God, inspired by confidence in Him. For Christians should acknowledge the sovereignty of the divine providence in ordering and overruling human institutions and relations for men's good. The way, therefore, to please God, to serve His will, and to experience His blessing, is for Christians not to be rebels against the prevailing order of society, but rather positively, submissively and dutifully to discharge the various responsibilities which the common relations of life put upon them. Christians should, therefore, be God-fearing, loyal and obedient citizens, considerate neighbours, diligent and faithful employees, uncomplaining victims of unjust treatment, dutiful and devoted wives or husbands, sympathetic and generous in personal relations, using every opportunity actively to forsake evil and to do good. Such living will be not only inherently good, but will also bring satisfaction to the individual Christian as his life is prospered by God's blessing.

a. Some reasons for self-discipline (ii. 11, 12)

There is here a twofold demand for disciplined and distinctive personal conduct as Christians. One half of the demand is negative and private, a demand for abstinence in personal living. The other half of the demand is positive and public, a demand for behaviour that is openly and recognizably virtuous in the eyes of men.

11. Three reasons are given why we should thus discipline and direct our lives, two of them in this verse. First, we are reminded of our heavenly citizenship. Once we become Christians we are to think of ourselves as only *strangers* (RV 'sojourners') *and pilgrims* on the earth (cf. i. 1; Heb. xi. 13), residing here temporarily, but not belonging, nor becoming settlers. The first word, *paroikoi*, describes those who have no rights or legal status in the place where they are merely sojourners. The second word, *parepidēmoi*, emphasizes that they are temporary residents only. So, as long as we are in this world, there should be in our lives as Christians a certain detachment. Second, such discipline is in the interests of our true well-being. Perils still beset our spiritual life from our fallen human nature. The flesh is a good servant, but a bad master. *Fleshly lusts*, by which are meant our selfish, indulgent and potentially vicious, natural appetites, are by their very nature like mutineers, capable of raising an insurrection and waging a campaign against our spiritual devotion. They wage war within against the true self (cf. Rom. vii. 23; Jas. iv. 1). By deliberate abstinence we must refuse to give them a foothold or taking-off ground.

12. The third reason for self-discipline is our influence for God on others. Our aim and prayer should be that our detractors should come to see that our *good works* are made possible only by the gracious working of God's Spirit, and so be brought to acknowledge their divine author. Here Peter is explicitly repeating teaching learnt from the Lord Himself (see Mt. v. 16).

The word *anastrophē*, translated *conversation*, refers to a man's whole conduct or 'behaviour' (RV). The adjective *kalos, honest* (as distinct from *agathos*, which is used with the same noun in iii. 16 and which also means 'good'), describes goodness which can be seen by others. The same adjective is used in Mt. v. 16, and appropriately recurs later in this verse in the phrase *by your good works. Whereas*; better, as in RV, 'wherein', i.e. in the actual behaviour which men refer to in order to speak against us, but which God will ultimately use to cause them to give Him the glory.

They speak against you as evildoers. Foul charges of immorality and criminal conduct were made against Christians by those out to run them down. Charges of this kind were, and still are, best answered or silenced not by words but by deeds (cf. ii. 15).

The verb *epopteuein*, translated *behold*, can convey the sense of seeing because one has been initiated, and has had one's eyes opened. Also the preposition *ek*, 'from' or 'out of' rather than *by*, suggests that this is a subsequent product of *your good works*. Their observers do not glorify God at the time, but may be led to do so later when they recognize the real character of the works and the divine help which alone made them possible. A *visitation* is a special drawing near of God to deal with men either in judgment or in mercy. The phrase might therefore refer to the final day of judgment, when such malicious detractors of God's people will have to give God the glory, and confess the truth concerning what they saw. Here, however, it more probably refers to the time in this life, when God may deal with such individuals to bring them to repentance and faith. What He will then use to cause them to change their attitude will be the 'good works' which they have seen and which they have hitherto deliberately misrepresented.

b. The duty of submission to the secular power (ii. 13–17)

The principle of submission to the divine ordering of human life applies, for instance, to the individual's proper recognition of the civil authorities. He should recognize that such rulers have a divinely-appointed responsibility to preserve law and order, to prevent anarchy and moral corruption, and to promote and encourage good conduct. This they do by taking action to punish the wrongdoer and to commend those whose conduct is virtuous and exemplary. The Christian citizen, therefore, ought to submit himself to their authority, and to be

warned or encouraged by what they do and say in the discharge of their public duty.

Such loyal submission to civil rulers is plainly God's will;
and such virtuous conduct may well serve to restrain the
words and deeds of those potential law-breakers, who themselves have neither the will nor the mind to be reasonably
law-abiding. As citizens Christians should neither forget that
they are free, nor be tempted to presume upon their God-given
freedom by using it wrongly as a kind of cover of evil. For,
paradoxically, the proper use for Christians to make of their
freedom is not to do as they like regardless of the demands of
the civil authorities, but to use it, as conscious and willing
bondslaves of God, by freely choosing to be law-abiding. Also,
such proper recognition of the truth about human life and its
divinely-ordered relationships means that Christians ought to
give every fellow human-being due respect as God's creature,
deliberately to engage in acts of love towards the Christian
brotherhood, and always to show reverence for God and
respect for the powers that be.

13a. In both AV and RV the words *anthrōpinē ktisis* are translated *ordinance of man*. RSV renders 'human institution'. In
classical Greek *ktisis* is used of the human founding of a city.
Here, therefore, the phrase may refer to the common social
institutions of ordered society (such as the state, the household,
or a local, social or industrial group, and the family). The
actual human arrangement of these may vary considerably
from place to place and from age to age. What Christians ought
to recognize is that in their general character such institutions
are in harmony with God's will for the ordering of human life;
and so they ought loyally to fulfil their proper duties in relation
to them. In biblical Greek, however, *ktisis* and the verb *ktizō*
are used exclusively of the products and activity of God, not
man. So *ktisis* is elsewhere rendered 'creation' (see Mk. xiii.
19), or 'creature' (see 2 Cor. v. 17). It is, therefore, probably
truer to biblical usage to understand the phrase here as
meaning 'every divine institution among men'—thus ascribing

the existence of such human institutions directly to the divine initiative (cf. 'The powers that be are ordained of God'; Rom. xiii. 1).

The exhortation to *submit yourselves . . . for the Lord's sake* stresses the deliberately chosen, voluntary character of the subjection. Christians should be dutiful not because they have to be so, but because they freely choose to be so. The compound verb *hupotassō* which is used here, meaning 'rank yourselves under', may be directly related in thought to the simple verb *tassō*, which is used to describe the divine ordaining in Rom. xiii. 1. Because God in His sovereignty has ordered human life so, Christians should fit into the divine arrangement and submissively fulfil their appointed functions. The phrase *for the Lord's sake* provides the proper Christian motive for such dutiful obedience or conformity. There are three possible interpretations: (i) because by faith Christians recognize such institutions as being divinely ordained, therefore they render their submission primarily to the Lord (cf. Heb. xii. 9, where *hupotassō* also occurs); (ii) because as Man, the Lord Himself was submissive, therefore Christians ought to follow His example; (iii) in order to commend to others Christ as Lord, and not to bring reproach on His name as well as on themselves by unruly behaviour, therefore obedience is enjoined.

13b, 14. The first example of such a divine institution for human life is found in the state or rather in the civil authorities, whether it be the supreme ruler or subordinate officials duly commissioned. If the strong biblical sense is given to *ktisis*, i.e. 'divine creation' (see RV mg.), then kings are to be regarded as being given their place and function by God. Also the provincial governors and other state officials are to be regarded not merely as deriving their authority by commission from the king, but rather as sharing in the divine commission, which in their case has been extended to them 'through' (*dia*; see RV mg.) the king.

Such civil rulers are explicitly commissioned to represent

God as the Judge. They give active expression to His righteousness and His wrath by inflicting just retribution on wrongdoers, and by publicly commending and rewarding those who do well (cf. Rom. xiii. 3, 4). All to whom such divine authority is thus delegated ought in its exercise to be like God, by whose commission and in whose service they act; i.e. they should love righteousness and hate iniquity (see Heb. i. 8, 9). This implies that the civil government is responsible not only for the citizens' material well-being, but also and most of all for their moral well-being. It is evident that this can be promoted and preserved only if vice is punished and virtue encouraged.

15. *So, houtōs*, may be understood as referring either backward or forward. The *will of God* is, first, that Christians should be subject to the civil government, and, second, that by their law-abiding behaviour they should avoid the condemnation and win the commendation of the civil authorities. The practical consequence then will be that by such virtuous behaviour they will silence, or prevent from speaking at all, those who, without any proper thought or knowledge, are otherwise all too ready to run Christians down. The verb *phimoun*, translated *put to silence*, means to 'muzzle'. The same verb is used to express what our Lord did when He 'put the Sadducees to silence' (Mt. xxii. 34); and what He said when He silenced an unclean spirit ('Hold thy peace', Mk. i. 25), and when He stilled the storm ('Be still', Mk. iv. 39). The word can cover the idea of preventing someone from speaking, as well as the idea of causing someone to cease from speaking. The word for *ignorance, agnōsia*, is a stronger word than *agnoia*, and indicates more than 'lack of knowledge'. It suggests possible obstinate unwillingness to learn or to accept the truth. The same word occurs in 1 Cor. xv. 34, 'some have no knowledge of God'. *Foolish men, hoi aphrones*, means those without reason, who are senseless in what they are prone to say about Christianity. The whole phrase refers to the kind of talkers who run Christianity down without either reason or knowledge. The assertion is that what will silence them is law-abiding conduct.

16. Christians should recognize and actively enjoy the freedom which is theirs in Christ, without abusing it. For example, it must not be made a cover or excuse for wrong-doing, particularly self-indulgence (cf. Gal. v. 13). Nor should they forget that they ought also to live as God's 'bondservants' (RV) or 'slaves' (Gk. *douloi*). 'The only true liberty, of which a dependent being like man is capable, is the free use of his faculties in the service of God'[1] (cf. 1 Cor. vii. 22).

Although subjection to men is enjoined it does not mean a denial of Christian freedom. Obedience should be rendered by the Christian not of necessity, but by glad and willing choice, and out of a sense of obligation to God rather than to men. This significant and radical difference in the spirit in which obedient service is to be rendered by Christians is strikingly illustrated by our Lord's injunctions in Mt. v. 39-41. The governing idea is that, when you have been compelled to submit, you should openly show that you are still free to choose by engaging in more of the same service willingly and on your own initiative.

17. To *honour*, or to 'esteem highly', is the proper general attitude to adopt towards all men. It is due equally to all as God's creatures, and as the objects of His peculiar love and care (see Gn. v. 1, ix. 6; Ps. viii. 4, 5; Pr. xiv. 31; Rom. xiv. 10; Jas. iii. 8-10). This principle condemns much of man's treatment of his fellows both in the political and in the industrial world. To *fear*, or to 'reverence', is the corresponding proper—and unique—attitude to God. These injunctions are governed by the general demand so to recognize the true character of different individuals and groups as to render to one and all appropriate regard and treatment.

To *love* is to be the distinctive Christian attitude towards the Christian community (cf. i. 22, iii. 8, iv. 8, v. 14). It is noteworthy here that Christians are particularly exhorted to express love not towards one another individually, but towards the Church as a distinct body or fellowship. On this point

[1] John Brown, Vol. ii, p. 14.

words to be found in the Westminster Confession are worthy of quotation and attention, the more so because they are nowadays so rarely read. 'All saints that are united to Jesus Christ their head by his Spirit, and by faith . . . (are) united to one another in love, they have communion in each other's gifts and graces; and are obliged to the performance of such duties, public and private, as do conduce to their mutual good, both in the inward and outward man. Saints, by profession, are bound to maintain an holy fellowship and communion in the worship of God, and in performing such other spiritual services as tend to their mutual edification; as also in relieving each other in outward things, according to their several abilities and necessities. Which communion, as God offereth opportunity, is to be extended unto all those who in every place call upon the name of the Lord Jesus.'[1] On this point, John Brown discerningly commented that 'mistaken apprehension as to what this brotherhood, or, in other words, what the Church of Christ is, has led into very important practical mistakes, and induced men, under the impression that they were loving and honouring the brotherhood, to hate and persecute the brethren. Men have often thought they were showing their regard to the Church by maltreating its true members.'[2]

c. The duty of servants to masters (ii. 18–21a)

Here Peter accepts slavery and the organization of society in households under despotic and autocratic heads as a prevailing human social arrangement or 'set-up', in which the Christian, who is a servant, should find and fill his place by active submission. It is the Christian's new awareness of God and of what is pleasing to Him, and his sense of his calling in Christ, that should inspire and enable him to do this, even when it is difficult and painful to stick to it in practice because of harsh masters and unjust treatment.

[1] Westminster Confession, xxvi, 1, 2.
[2] Vol. ii, p. 99.

18. *Oiketai, servants,* means members of a household, domestic servants, including freemen as well as slaves. What Peter has primarily in mind is not slaves as a class, but the household as a common social institution. *Despotai, masters,* is a strong word, denoting 'absolute ownership and uncontrolled power'. *With all fear* may mean (as in Eph. vi. 5) out of respect for their position as masters (cf. 'honour the king', ii. 17), or much more probably, out of reverence for God and His sovereign control and providential ordering of the circumstances of men's lives (cf. Col. iii. 22).

Masters, it is recognized, may be of two distinct kinds. Some are *good and gentle* or 'considerate'. The second word, *epieikēs,* means fundamentally 'fair' or 'reasonable'. It also is interpreted as meaning 'yielding' or 'ready to forgo one's rights'; and so 'content to take less than one's due' (Aristotle). In the LXX it is used of God as 'ready to forgive' (Ps. lxxxvi. 5). Other masters may be *froward.* The Greek word *skolios* means literally 'curved', 'bent', 'not straight' (see Lk. iii. 5). Used metaphorically of people it means 'crooked' (see Phil. ii. 15), 'perverse', 'unfair', and so 'awkward to deal with'.

19, 20. Peter encourages uncomplaining persistence in submissive loyalty even when it involves the painful endurance of unjust treatment. There is no credit, he says, in submitting to being cuffed (the word is *kolaphizomenoi,* 'struck with the fist'), nothing to bring one fame or *glory* in taking punishment manfully, when one has done wrong. It is the patient uncomplaining submission to suffering when one has done well that is *acceptable with God.*

What Peter actually twice declares is that such action has about it the quality of *charis,* 'grace'. Verse 19 begins, *touto gar charis,* 'for this is grace', and verse 20 ends, *touto charis para Theō,* 'this is grace with God'. What does he mean? The word can describe something pleasing to look upon, or graceful in appearance. Usually in the Bible it describes both an undeserved act of kindness, a favour, and the appreciation, thanks, or gratitude, it should call forth in return. Peter

probably had in mind our Lord's own teaching recorded in
Lk. vi. 32–34. There three times the question is asked, 'What
thank (*charis*) have ye?' where the sense may simply be, 'How
are you deserving any thanks or reward?' (cf. Lk. xvii. 9;
Mt. v. 46). However, because such gratitude is only properly
due when something not due is first given in pure grace, the
question may embrace in thought both movements, *viz.*, what
grace is there in such action? and so what gratitude is due to
you for it? Here, in 1 Peter, it is possible to read all three
meanings of *charis* into the full sense, *viz.*, such action is pleasing
in God's eyes because it is an expression of grace and deserving,
therefore, of gratitude; i.e. because it is gratuitous it is thankworthy.

Such action, as Peter goes on to indicate, corresponds in
principle to the action of Christ. This is how He behaved when
He had to endure suffering which He did not deserve. He
took it patiently, in silent submission. Such action was pleasing
in God's sight. It was an expression of divine grace. It won
God's approval and reward. It was for our profit. It furthered
our salvation. In thus acting He provided a pattern of
behaviour which we are meant closely to follow. For this is
how God is pleased, grace is manifested, divine commendation
is obtained, and men previously hostile are moved to acknowledge God. Nor can we argue that this teaching does not
concern us since slavery is a thing of the past. There are in life
comparable positions in business or in a household, in college
and indeed in the Church, in which others are set over us. It
is then our Christian calling to be submissive, co-operative and
uncomplaining, even if pained by unfair treatment.

For conscience toward God. The noun *suneidēsis*, followed here
by the genitive 'of God', without a preposition, is best understood in the sense of 'consciousness' (cf. 1 Cor. viii. 7; Heb.
x. 2). The whole phrase, therefore, means prompted by a
conscious awareness of God's presence and will. Such a man
knows that God sees, and knows what God expects. His
concern is to please Him (cf. Eph. vi. 7).

21a. *For even hereunto were ye called* refers to the divine call in Christ to become members of His people. The complementary truth to be realized is that this calling is divinely intended to find its immediate earthly outworking in circumstances and relationships and experiences of the kind just mentioned. If, for instance, a slave becomes a Christian, it is normally an essential part of God's immediate purpose that he should now not cease to be a slave because he has become a Christian, but rather that he should glorify God by beginning to behave in relation to his master as only a Christian slave would (cf. I Cor. vii. 17–24).

d. The example of Christ our Redeemer (ii. 21b–25)

The surprising truth that God has appointed that the innocent should sometimes have to suffer here on earth as though they had done wrong, and the proper submissive spirit in which such suffering should consequently be endured, are both supremely illustrated in the passion of Christ. He has provided an example to be followed. For He was completely sinless both in deed and word. He endured unjust reproach and ill-treatment in silence, satisfied to commit Himself to God, the righteous Judge. In His case, too, it was the penalty due to our sins that He bore, right up to the extreme limit of public execution as though He were the worst of criminals. By this suffering He has brought to wandering and lost sinners deliverance and healing, restoration and the possibility of a new life dominated by new standards, and above all by a new attachment and devotion to Him.

21b. Christ Himself had taught His disciples three things about suffering: first, that He must suffer, because He was the Christ (Lk. xxiv. 25–27, 44–47); second, that His suffering was for others, to provide for the many a ransom and remission of sins (Mt. xx. 28, xxvi. 28); third, that all who would follow Him must similarly be prepared to suffer (Mk. viii. 34, x. 38, 39). At first Peter did not welcome or understand such teaching. Here, in this Epistle, he shows how completely he had himself come both to accept and to propagate such teaching as the very essentials of what we rightly call Christianity.

These three points are all significantly summed up together in this verse:

First, the implication of the phrase *because Christ also suffered* is that suffering is part of our calling only because it was first part of His. Suffering was divinely appointed for the Christ. So the inspired prophets had foreseen (i. 10–12).

Second, His suffering was not on His own account, but *for us*, i.e. on behalf of, and for the benefit of, others, to secure their redemption from sin (see verse 24).

Third, He thus provided in principle a precedent and an *example* for His followers. Suffering is something in which all who would in this present world be associated with God's Christ, and be called 'Christians', must expect to share. It is a prospect to be deliberately faced; and an experience to be regarded not with shame and resentment, but with joy and thanksgiving to God (see iv. 13, 16). The word *hupogrammos, example,* means something written underneath to be traced or copied over. The verb translated *ye should follow* is a compound one, *epakolouthein,* suggesting 'to follow closely upon', i.e. to tread in His steps. In relation to what Peter here confesses cf. Jn. xiii. 7, 15, 36, xxi. 18, 19, 22.

In verses 22–25 there is a remarkable use by Peter of Old Testament language. There are no less than five quotations or echoes of the statements and phraseology of Is. liii. Verse 22 follows Is. liii. 9; 'because he had done no violence, neither was any deceit in his mouth'. Verse 23 is parallel to Is. liii. 7; 'he was afflicted, yet he opened not his mouth'. Verse 24 has phraseology from Is. liii. 12; 'he bare the sin of many', and from Is. liii. 5; 'with his stripes we are healed'. Verse 25 echoes Is. liii. 6; 'All we like sheep have gone astray'. Even Peter, who had been an eyewitness of the sufferings of Jesus, and had himself heard the personal teaching of our Lord, knew no better language than this with which to describe some of the features and significance of Christ's passion. Such an example confirms Christians in the conviction that Old Testament prophecies and types were divinely provided, and are divinely intended to help men to understand and appreciate the Person and work of Christ.

22. This verse provides noteworthy testimony to the complete sinlessness of Jesus by one who had been on the closest terms of intimacy with Him. Jesus failed, asserts Peter, neither in deed nor word. He was not guilty either of error or deceit. This means, in a way which is true of no one else, that Jesus did not deserve to suffer. He was as a lamb without blemish and without spot (i. 19). And so, having no sin of His own for which to answer, He could bear the sin of others.

23. The stress here is on the surprising silence of Jesus, on His unprotesting submission to treatment which He did not personally deserve, because of His confidence in the righteousness and vindication of God. When unjustly reproached, He did not answer back. When unfairly treated He did not condemn His oppressors nor invoke judgment upon them (contrast Acts xxiii. 2, 3). This was something remarkable indeed. To such lengths does His example of patient submission go. Though the wording here is different, this corresponds to yet another point in the prophetic depiction of the suffering servant of the Lord in Is. liii. There (verse 7) it is twice stressed that He kept His mouth shut, *viz.*, 'He was oppressed, and he was afflicted, yet he opened not his mouth: he is brought as a lamb to the slaughter, and as a sheep before her shearers is dumb, so he openeth not his mouth'. Here the Greek present participles and imperfect tenses emphasize that under sustained and repeated provocation, never once did He break the silence. All the time during which He was the victim of abuse, He was not reviling back. All the time during which He was suffering, He was not resorting to threats.

The verb *paradidōmi*, 'to hand over', is used of our Lord's betrayal into the hands of wicked men (see Mt. xxvi. 14–16; Mk. xiv. 41, 42). It is used of John the Baptist being 'delivered up' or 'cast into prison' (Mt. iv. 12). It is used of our Lord being 'delivered' to Pilate by the Jews, and of Pilate 'delivering' Him to the soldiers—in each case for punishment, as if He were a wrongdoer (see Jn. xix. 11, 16). Here in the phrase *committed himself* it is used to describe our Lord's own surrender of Himself to bear the penalty of sin—not His own sin but ours (cf. Rom. iv. 25), and not at the hands of men, but at the hands of God, the righteous Judge.

Here we may see, first, the true character and the inspiring confidence of Christ's willing, uncomplaining submission to unjust suffering. He acknowledged above His earthly circumstances and oppressors the sovereignty and the righteous judgment of God, and He committed Himself and His cause into God's hands. By so doing He provided in principle and in spirit an example to be followed by all who, in following Him, find that they, too, have to suffer unjustly. They should, as Peter says (in iv. 19, RV), 'commit their souls in well-doing unto a faithful Creator'.

Also, in this the unique instance of our Lord's passion, when the sinless One suffered as if He were the worst of sinners, and bore the extreme penalty of sin, there is a double sense in which He may have acknowledged God as the righteous Judge. On the one hand, because voluntarily, and in fulfilment of God's will, He was taking the sinner's place and bearing sin, He did not protest at what He had to suffer. Rather He consciously recognized that it was the penalty righteously due to sin. So He handed Himself over to be punished. He recognized that in letting such shame, pain and curse fall upon Him, the righteous God was judging righteously. On the other hand, because He Himself was sinless, He also believed that in due time God, as the righteous Judge, would vindicate Him as righteous, and exalt Him from the grave, and reward Him for what He had willingly endured for others' sake by giving Him the right completely to save them from the penalty and power of their own wrongdoing.

24. The statement *who his own self bare our sins in his own body on the tree* explicitly confirms the two ideas that the suffering He endured was the penalty due to sin, but that the sins whose penalty He thus bore were not His own but ours. He thus took the place of sinners, and in their stead bore the punishment due to their sin. What happened to Him was penal; and the function which He fulfilled was in some sense substitutionary, or instead of others to whom the penalty was due. 'To bear sin' or 'iniquity' means in the Old Testament to be answerable for it, and to endure its penalty, e.g. to die (see Ex. xxviii. 43; Lv. xxiv. 15, 16). This is the phraseology used in Is. liii. 12, 'He bare the sin of many'.

The description here is spectacular and dramatic. Peter is giving his testimony as an eyewitness to an event in history. This deed to save sinners was wrought out by Christ Himself, none other, He did it here on earth, in flesh and blood, in His own body as Man. He carried sin, and submitted to their its penalty, right up on to the tree (see RV mg. The preposition *epi* followed by the accusative case suggests motion towards a destination). This means that He went through with His appointed and chosen task of suffering for us, or bearing our sins, right up to the climax of bearing the extreme penalty of capital punishment and public execution by crucifixion or hanging on a tree. Thus in men's reckoning He was treated as the worst of criminals and sent to the most shameful and painful form of death men knew; and in God's reckoning by such exposure He came openly and publicly under the curse of heaven (see Dt. xxi. 22, 23).

It is particularly noteworthy that in a context in which Peter is primarily concerned to exhort his readers to follow Christ's example and patiently endure unjust treatment, once he has introduced the subject of Christ's suffering, he cannot refrain from giving explicit mention of its unique atoning character, and he deliberately changes the reference from the second to the first person plural (*viz.*, '*our* sins'), in order to include himself among the sinners in whose stead Christ endured sin's full and extreme penalty.

The purpose of Christ's passion is to bring to those for whom He suffered, complete separation from their sins, and the possibility of a new life of righteousness. Paradoxically it is through the hurt done to Him that they get healing. The positive interest here is not just in sinners securing release from the guilt and penalty of their sins, but rather in what this makes possible—complete emancipation from sin and sinning, and the redirection of the life towards God and His righteousness. The verb *apoginesthai, being dead,* occurs nowhere else in the Greek Bible. It means literally 'to be away' or 'removed from', 'to depart'; and the participle here used is found in classical Greek writers to describe 'the departed', i.e. 'the dead'. Here the word describes what sinners are to become in relation to their sins, because Christ bore these sins for them (cf. iv. 1; Rom. vi. 2, 11). The idea is that, Christ having died for sins, and to sin, as our proxy or substitute, our consequent standing before God is that of those who have no more connection with our old sins, or with the life of sinning. Henceforth we are free, and are intended, to live unto righteousness (cf. iv. 2; Rom. vi. 11–13, 18).

The phrase *by whose stripes ye were healed* is taken from Is. liii. 5. The word *mōlōps, stripes,* means a bruise, scar or weal, left by a lash. It describes a physical condition with which slaves were all too familiar. It recalls the scourging of Jesus. The introduction of this phrase confirms that Peter's thought here, however paradoxical, is deliberately that of benefit to be gained by sinners from our Lord's suffering in their stead. Here, as Theodore said, is 'a new and strange method of healing; the doctor suffered the cost, and the sick received the healing'.

25. The opening phraseology of this verse follows Is. liii. 6. It describes the general condition of humanity. Men are all prone to wander and go astray, like silly sheep, which describes the condition of Peter's readers before their conversion, i.e. what *ye were. Now* things are different. Life that lacked a guide, a guardian, and a goal, is now redirected both in dependence and devotion towards One who cares for their well-being by constant provision and supervision.

Returned unto, epestraphēte epi, suggests there has been in their lives a 'turning round' and a turning 'towards'. Their lives have ceased to be aimless and wandering and are redirected and dominated by a new personal attachment, just as a sheep's wandering and lost condition is ended by restored relation to the shepherd. In the phrase *the Shepherd and Bishop of your souls* the word *Bishop, episkopos,* is not a second title so much as a description of the function of the Shepherd, i.e. to be an 'overseer', to exercise oversight or pastoral care over the flock. Similarly, in principle, 'pastor' and 'bishop' are not two distinct offices, but alternative names for men called to the same kind of ministry in the Church of God. So Peter exhorts elders or presbyters to function both as shepherds and bishops (v. 1, 2); and Paul exhorts 'bishops' (whom Luke describes as elders or presbyters of the church) to function as pastors (Acts xx. 17, 28).

Peter's statement here implies (what was explicitly taught by our Lord, Jn. x. 16) that what unites those previously scattered abroad into one united flock is attachment to the one Shepherd (cf. ii. 4, 5). It also implies that in the Church the only 'chief Shepherd' (v. 4), and the one supreme, indispensable Bishop, is Christ Himself, not some other earthly Pope or Primate.

e. The duties of wives and husbands (iii. 1–7)

Marriage is another of God's ordinances for human society bringing individuals into mutual relations of responsibility. Peter here deals with the duties towards their married partners, first of Christian wives, and then of Christian husbands. It is important to notice, particularly in a day when classes in society all tend to assert their rights and to demand from others what they think is due to them, that what is here emphasized, in each case, are the duties to be discharged in relation to others. Clearly becoming a Christian should radically influence a person's behaviour in every social relationship, and not least in the sphere of the family. Here the individual's awareness that God's eye is upon him, and his sense of what is valued in God's sight, should determine how he acts. It goes without saying that this applies to women as much as to men.

1. *Likewise,* or 'similarly', links the new section on to what precedes, as part of the same series of exhortations concerning Christian living in relation to one's fellow-men in which the same principle of dutiful submission or rendering proper honour and respect is enforced (cf. ii. 13, 17, 18, iii. 7).

Wives are told to *be in subjection* or to 'submit' to their own husbands. This does not inculcate or imply the sexual inferiority of women. The subordination enjoined is one of function as a wife, mother, hostess, etc., within the sphere of the home. Every family, if it is to be united and to run happily, must have a head, just as a team must have a captain. The proper head of the family is the man. Final responsibility for decisions concerning what is done, and how or when it is done, must be his. The characteristic, therefore, desirable in a good wife is ready compliance with the responsible decisions and consequent practical demands of her husband. Indeed, this passage and context suggest that, just as some masters may be perverse (ii. 18), so some husbands, particularly non-Christian husbands, may be difficult and exacting to please. It is in such circumstances that the Christian wife's faith and devotion as a Christian should help and inspire her still to render submissive co-operation as a good wife.

The situation is envisaged of a Christian wife and an unbelieving husband, presumably a family originally totally heathen from which the wife only has so far become a Christian. The possibility is recognized that some non-Christian husbands may even be actively hostile to the gospel. The verb *apeithein,* here rendered *obey not,* is a strong word meaning to 'disobey', and is probably intended to describe husbands who, far from being won by hearing the gospel preached, deliberately set themselves against the truth.

Such a non-Christian husband may be won to accept the faith, so Peter suggests, by the silent witness of his wife's Christian conduct. In the phrase *without the word,* in contrast to the previous *obey not the word,* the noun 'word', *logos,* has no article. Whereas with the article *the word* refers to the gospel, the Christian message preached, 'without word' simply means without speaking or explaining, i.e. by the witness of conduct only. *Conversation, anastrophē,* means, not speech, but 'behaviour' (RV) or 'manner of life' (RV mg.). What is clearly implied here is that the wife gives her distinctive Christian witness to her husband, not by preaching at him, but by living before him, and particularly by being a good wife in her relation to him. This is how social superiors and intimate relatives, with whom Christians are in constant contact, are best reached with Christian witness. *They may . . . be won* (RV 'gained'). The verb is unqualified, and is capable of varied application. A husband thus converted to Christ is also 'gained' by himself, by his wife, and by the Church.

2. *While they behold* translates an aorist participle; the sense is rather 'because they have seen'. *Epopteuein* means 'to watch attentively', 'to see for oneself'. What such a non-Christian husband will have plenty of unsought opportunity to observe is that his wife's chaste bearing and behaviour are 'in fear', *en phobō,* i.e. inspired and determined by her reverence for God.

3, 4. A Christian wife should also seek to please God, and be a witness for Him, by her distinctive interest in conduct rather than in clothes, and particularly by cultivating and expressing a calm and imperturbable spirit, placid and gentle in relation to both people and circumstances. This will reveal that her behaviour is governed by a new standard of values, and by the deliberate choice and cultivation of characteristics highly esteemed in God's sight rather than in the eyes of other men or other women. For women naturally set great store by their outward appearance, and so give much attention to such matters as hair-style, jewellery and dress. The Christian woman, however, should remember that whereas 'man looketh on the outward appearance, the Lord looketh on the heart' (see 1 Sa. xvi. 7). It is the condition or attitude of one's inner disposition which matters to Him.

Note the dramatic description of the whole time-taking and expensive process of *outward adorning* (Gk., *kosmos*), *viz.*, plaiting the hair, setting jewels around one's neck, etc., and putting on garments. In the phrase *hidden man of the heart* the word *anthropos* refers to the human personality or person, the inner character (cf. Rom. vii. 22), unseen by others, which is not, like clothes or hair, an object of laboured external array and superficial display. In the original the adjective *not corruptible* has no noun. Some word like *ornament* (AV) or 'apparel' (RV) is best understood. *Aphthartos*, 'incorruptible', is a favourite word of this writer (see i. 4, 23). Here, as in i. 4 (cf. i. 18; Mt. vi. 19, 20), it describes a freedom from the decay or theft to which earthly treasures of the external material kind are all exposed. The contrast which Peter develops between *outward* and *hidden*, and between visible to men and seen by God, together with the deeper enduring spiritual values thereby emphasized, is in principle directly parallel to our Lord's teaching in Mt. vi. 1–18.

Meek describes the way in which such a wife submits to her husband's demands and intrusions by docile and gentle co-operation. *Quiet* describes her complementary and constant attitude, and the character of her action or reaction towards her husband and towards life in general. She shows no sign of rebellion or resentment, fuss or flurry.

5, 6. The outstanding wives of Old Testament times, particularly Abraham's wife Sarah, are introduced as an example or parallel to inspire Christian wives. These women enjoyed a privileged status as members of God's chosen people; they were *holy*. They learnt for themselves to make the God of Israel their confidence and hope. They displayed some outworked holiness in their behaviour. Their lives were adorned by those desirable characteristics of personal conduct, particularly in relation to their husbands, namely, submission, active well-doing and freedom from panic and alarm. In particular, Sarah showed a wife's proper deference to Abraham, acknowledging him as her master. It is her children that

women who become Christians are in status, and are called to
become in outworked character by emulating her dutifulness
and by persisting in well-doing and in unperturbed quietness.

The RV mg. shows that some translators treat the reference
to Sarah and to becoming her children as a parenthesis, thus
connecting the Greek participles at the end of verse 6 with 'the
holy women' of verse 5. This gives a coherence and complete-
ness to the reference to these women, because they are then
said to exhibit the same three characteristics as the previous
verses have indicated that good Christian wives should possess,
namely, submissiveness, well-doing and freedom from panic.
Though, seeing that the chief purpose of the passage is to
exhort Christian wives to reproduce such virtues, the AV and
RV renderings do effectively convey the ultimate sense and
challenge of the reference to Sarah and those like her; and
they may also express more exactly how the syntax of the
Greek sentence should be understood.

Calling him lord means acknowledging him, with due deference, as her husband or master. This phraseology is similar and
comparable to the description of the believer as one who
confesses or calls upon Christ as Lord. Such a confession of
relationship is properly completed by obedience or dutiful
submission. *Whose daughters (tekna,* RV 'children') *ye are,* or you
have become, i.e. whose true descendants you show yourselves
to be. Just as Abraham is called the father of the faithful, so
Sarah may be described as the mother of the obedient.
Amazement, RV 'terror', translates the Greek *ptoēsis,* meaning
'alarm', 'agitation'. The word may be either a cognate or an
objective accusative (see AV and RV); i.e. 'terror' may describe
either the kind of fear which might be felt, or the alarm which
might be feared.

Possibly there is in these verses 3–6 a somewhat distant echo
of Pr. iii. 25–27. Certainly the predominant exhortation of
that passage re-echoes a main theme of this Epistle. For Peter
seeks to encourage Christians, whatever their circumstances
and experience, to fulfil before God the obligations of their

position in society in relation to their fellow-men, and thus to continue actively to do good, without fear or alarm at threats or ill-treatment, because of their quiet confidence and steadfast hope in God (cf. ii. 12, 15, 23, iii. 13, 14, iv. 19).

7. Peter now deals with the Christian husband's corresponding duty to his wife. There is no suggestion here that such a wife might be a non-Christian. Contrast the reference in verse 1 to the non-Christian husband of a believing wife.

The Christian husband should let all his living together with his wife be informed and guided by a proper awareness of her condition in relation to himself both in nature and grace. On the one hand, naturally, he should recognize her more limited physical powers as a woman, and should give her corresponding consideration and protection. Only so will he render her due honour and be worthy of her marital confidence and devotion. On the other hand, spiritually, he should also recognize their full equality as fellow-sharers in the grace of God, and in His gift to them both of eternal life. He should, therefore, live with her as a man fully aware that, in addition to the natural enjoyment of each other, they are, as Christians, called together to a spiritual fellowship with God and Christ, a sphere in which his wife is not weaker or inferior, but a joint-heir. Only if this delicately balanced fellowship between husband and wife is thus properly maintained will their union reach its true Christian fulfilment. For such a partnership is meant to be specially fruitful, not only physically in having children, but also spiritually in praying together and in seeing prayer answered (cf. Mt. xviii. 19; 1 Cor. vii. 3–5). So care should be exercised that their prayers are not 'cut into' (*enkoptesthai*). Human disharmony can upset spiritual co-operation.

Dwell with them according to knowledge. The verb *sunoikein*, to dwell together, is often used in the LXX of marital intercourse as in Hebrew is the verb 'to know' (see Gn. iv. 1, and in Gk., Mt. i. 25). What should restrain the Christian husband and wife from unworthy sexual indulgence, and what they should prize and pursue more than physical marital union, is the knowledge of God (see 1 Thes. iv. 3–5; Jn. xvii. 3).

f. Principles of Christian living (iii. 8–12)

This main section of the Epistle (ii. 11–iii. 12), in which Peter deals with Christian living in relation to one's fellow-men, is now concluded with an exhortation, which applies (like the opening words in ii. 11–17) to all classes alike. He exhorts them to show Christian love, kindness and goodwill towards others, particularly, on the one hand, towards fellow-Christians, and, on the other hand, towards the unfriendly and hostile. He quotes from the Old Testament (Ps. xxxiv) to enforce the truth that true enjoyment of life, and the accompanying experience of God's help and care rather than His opposition, depend upon the individual's active rejection of evil and his pursuit of good, particularly in his dealings with his fellow-men.

8. The force of the phrase *to de telos, finally* (lit. 'now the end'), is 'to sum up', or possibly, to bring to the end or climax by adding the crowning point. It does not indicate the intention to end the Epistle, but rather to sum up and complete the preceding exhortations to different classes by brief practical exhortations applicable to all, and simply demanding love in action.

This verse lists five characteristics desirable in Christians. It is worthy of note that they are all social, and have to do with Christians' relations to one another. *Of one mind, homophrones*, means 'minding the same things'. Note the use of the corresponding verb 'to mind' in Mk. viii. 33, RV (AV 'savourest'), and Rom. viii. 5. A man's character is determined and revealed by the things to which he gives his mind. Christians, Peter insists, should be united by a common interest and outlook; they should all 'mind' the things of God and of the Spirit, and thus imitate the mind of Christ (cf. Phil. ii. 2, 5). Just as Christians have a common 'confession' (*homologia*; see Heb. iii. 1, iv. 14, RV), i.e. they all say the same thing, so they should have a common mind, a mind informed by God's Word and Spirit. What Peter describes and desires, therefore, is not just human agreement together, but agreement reached by each and all receiving the truth of God (cf. Eph. iv. 13–15).

The word *sumpatheis, having compassion,* means 'suffering together', having responsive fellow-feelings, e.g. rejoicing with those that rejoice, and weeping with those that weep (Rom. xii. 15; cf. Heb. xiii. 3). At its deepest level this should follow the preceding characteristic. Those who are united by a common spiritual mind, should be moved by, or be sensitive to, the same spiritual emotions. This is why Christians can unite with fervour in singing hymns which confess the faith, or give God praise, etc.

Love as brethren, philadelphoi, implies loving one another because we are now related as fellow-members of God's family. Again, it is the Godward reference that gives the word its deepest and distinctive Christian meaning (cf. 1 Thes. iv. 9).

Be pitiful, eusplagchnoi, RV 'tenderhearted', means being affectionately sensitive, quick to feel and to show affection. The Greek word refers to the good condition of a man's 'inward parts' or 'bowels' (see Phil. ii. 1). While the Greeks associated these with courage (cf. our colloquial use of 'guts'), so that to them this adjective might mean 'brave-hearted', the Hebrews associated them with feeling or affection. Here, therefore, the adjective means 'tenderhearted'. The corresponding verb is used only of Christ in the New Testament; so only as we have His Spirit can we become 'tenderhearted'. In our day, with so much tragic news broadcast so frequently and so widely, we have become too accustomed to hear of other people's sufferings, and so tend to be superficially hardened and not so easily or so deeply moved; or we do nothing about it. There is all the more need for the free, full and practical expression of such deep feeling among Christian brethren, issuing in corresponding action.

Be courteous translates *philophrones,* 'friendly'. The preferable reading, followed by RV, is *tapeinophrones,* 'humbleminded'. Humility or lowliness of mind is a peculiarly biblical virtue, not appreciated as such by the Greeks. Such an attitude corresponds to the facts of life. We are weak, dependent, finite creatures, with bodies of 'humiliation' or 'lowliness' (Phil. iii. 21, RV). This, therefore, is the right spirit in which to live before God. It was the spirit exhibited and inculcated by Jesus (Mt. xi. 29). It is the spirit which God rewards—with sustaining grace and consequent exaltation (v. 5, 6).

9. Peter now indicates how Christians should act towards the unfriendly, towards any who maliciously do them harm or run them down. The governing principles of Christian action in such circumstances were explicitly taught by Jesus Himself. On the one hand, there should be no retaliation, no treating others as they treat us. On the other hand, there should be a positive expression in word and deed of active goodwill. Such behaviour, in direct opposition to what seems natural to men, is the kind of behaviour to which we are called in Christ, and which will bring its own rewarding issue in an increase of the enjoyment in our own lives of similar treatment at God's hand. For He, too, is full of active goodwill towards those who have sinned against Him both in deed and word (see Mt. v. 44, 45; Lk. vi. 27, 28, 35, 36).

Not rendering evil for evil. The verb *apodidonai* means to give back in return, to render as due. An identical injunction occurs both in Rom. xii. 17 and 1 Thes. v. 15. Obviously it was a regular part of the ethical instruction given to converts, instruction based, as Jesus had commanded, on what He Himself had taught (see Mt. xxviii. 19, 20). *But contrariwise blessing.* The word here, *eulogountes*, is a participle not a noun. So Jesus had taught: 'Bless them that curse you' (Mt. v. 44; Lk. vi. 28). So Paul described his apostolic behaviour: 'Being reviled, we bless' (1 Cor. iv. 12). The verb *eulogein*, 'to bless', includes the ideas of speaking well of those who speak ill of us, showing them active kindness, i.e. bestowing blessings upon them, and praying God's blessing upon them.

The phrase 'hereunto were ye called' (RV) repeats the language of ii. 21. There the reference was to the patient endurance of unjust treatment; here it is to the active re-compense of good for evil. In Christ God blesses those who have sinned against Him. It is therefore an essential part of our Christian calling ourselves to experience the kind of treatment which we are here exhorted to give to those who sin against us. Indeed, we shall enter increasingly into the full enjoyment of the *blessing* of God's forgiveness and goodwill only if we learn ourselves to extend similar forgiveness and goodwill to others (see Mt. vi. 12, 14, 15, xviii. 32–35; Mk. xi. 25, 26). The inspiration of such conduct should be found in the recollection of God's treatment of us (see Eph. iv. 32). Christians, therefore, should behave in this way not only for the cold, moral reason that the highest law of God enjoins it, but also for the warm, personal and theological reason that our own enjoyment as sinners of the divine mercy demands it; we can rightly do no other. Note that we determine the measure of the blessing we ourselves experience by the extent to which we obey such teaching (see Lk. vi. 36–38).

10. Peter provides apt scriptural completion and confirmation of his exhortation to abstain from retaliation in deed or word, and to treat the unfriendly with kindness, by quoting Ps. xxxiv. 12–16. It has been suggested that sections of this psalm were used in the early Church, as part of a catechism or hymn. To give up evil in word and deed, to do what is good, to seek to establish and to maintain peaceful relations with one's fellows is the way to enjoy true and satisfying life.

In quoting Ps. xxxiv. 12 Peter adapts the phraseology. What he here writes does not, as in the psalm, describe simply the man who desires a long life and a good one. Rather it describes the man who wishes to live a life which he can love and find worth while, a life that is not marked by endless frustration or boredom. Contrast Ec. ii. 17: 'Therefore I hated life; because the work that is wrought under the sun is grievous unto me: for all is vanity and vexation of spirit', or 'a striving after wind' (RV).

Let him refrain translates *pausatō*, meaning 'let him make to cease'. The kind of words to be given up are those that are either malicious (i.e. calculated to harm) or deceitful (i.e. calculated to mislead). Note that it is their effect on others that is in mind (cf. Ex. xx. 16).

11. *Let him eschew* (RV 'turn away from') *evil*. Wrongdoing is a course of action which, by deliberate choice and self-control, is to be quitted. *Good* is not something just to be spoken of with admiration, but something to be done. Happy and harmonious relations with others are not only to be sought but zealously pursued (cf. Rom. xii. 18, xiv. 19; Heb. xii. 14).

12. *The Lord*, i.e. in Ps. xxxiv. 15, 16, 'the LORD', Jehovah, the God who has entered into covenant relation with His people. He it is who watches over the righteous. He exercises active oversight and care over them. He is alert to hear and to heed their 'supplication' (RV) or request, their confession of need. On the other hand, He sees, and must show His judgment and punishment towards *them that do evil*. The use here of the name *Lord* for God possibly implies that His covenant people are especially in mind. When they do evil they are bound to encounter His displeasure and His discipline (cf. Am. iii. 1, 2; Ho. xii. 2).

VI. SUFFERING FOR RIGHTEOUSNESS' SAKE
(iii. 13–17)

Since those who set themselves to do good have God on their side (iii. 11, 12), there is no-one who can really do them ill (cf. Rom. viii. 31). But in this world it is always possible that Christians may have to suffer for righteousness' sake. This may be God's will for them. When it is, they should regard such suffering, not as their unhappy lot, but as an added privilege. It certainly is no occasion either for alarm or for distress, not to say for apostasy. In such circumstances they should maintain true heart reverence for Christ as Lord and be ready openly to confess their Christian hope. They should take care not to deserve suffering as evildoers, but by their conscientious and consistent good conduct should put their detractors to shame.

13. Peter begins this section by pointing out that, for Christians living as they ought, the likelihood of suffering is small. Such a way of life is generally free from the opposition of men. If you prove yourselves enthusiasts for good, Peter asks, who is likely to ill-treat you? Certainly magistrates, if they are doing their duty, exist for the commendation, not the persecution, of those who do well (ii. 14). Such seems to be the obvious meaning of this verse.

Yet in its context, and as a challenge addressed to Christians, the question may have deeper implications. For Peter immediately goes on to speak of the possibility of suffering on account of righteousness; in doing so, he was only reiterating the teaching of our Lord, who warned His disciples that they might be persecuted for righteousness' sake (Mt. v. 10–12; cf. 2 Tim. iii. 12). It does not seem possible, therefore, to assert without reservation that followers of Christ who seek to do good will be free from opposition and consequent hardship. What Peter asks is, *Who is he that will harm you?* The verb *kakōun* may mean not only 'to ill-treat' or 'to distress', but also, which is appropriate here, to damage through such ill-treatment. It is used in Acts vii. 6, 'entreat them evil'; and in Acts xii. 1, 'vex' (RV 'afflict'). In its context the question may mean, as the AV translation suggests: No matter what physical suffering or material hardship you may have to encounter, who can do you any real evil if you are actively doing good?

Not only so; those who thus seek to do good, as the quotation from Ps. xxxiv has just confirmed, have God to watch over them. God can be counted on in His righteousness not only to answer their cry for help, but also to set His face against evildoers. How then can anyone do them evil, if God Himself is active to help them, and to oppose the evildoer? (cf. Rom. viii. 31,35–37). *Followers* translates *mimētai*, 'imitators'. The preferable reading, followed by RV, is *zēlōtai*, 'zealous devotees of', 'enthusiasts for'. The phrase *ean genēsthe, if ye be,* means 'if you become'.

14. The Greek underlying *but and if ye suffer* expresses a remote possibility, i.e. 'even if you should suffer'. Peter asserts that any who thus suffer *for righteousness' sake* are *happy* (Gk. *makarioi*, 'blessed'). This reiterates our Lord's explicit teaching in Mt. v. 10–12. It is, of course, paradoxical, the exact opposite of men's natural opinion and reaction. To be 'happy' in this sense, does not mean to 'feel delighted' but to be 'highly privileged', the objects of special divine favour (cf. Mary's confession, 'All generations shall call me blessed', Lk. i. 48). By contrast, when men have to suffer, their natural reaction is not only to feel unhappy, but also to regard themselves as underprivileged, unfairly treated, and objects of God's neglect or ill-treatment.

Be not afraid of their terror is more literally, as in RV, 'fear not their fear', i.e. either the fear which they experience, or the fear which they instil. Peter here follows some of the phrases and ideas of Is. viii. 12, 13: 'Neither fear ye their fear, nor be afraid. Sanctify the LORD of hosts himself; and let him be your fear.' There the meaning is, 'Do not share their fear'; and 'fear' is possibly used in verse 12, as well as in verse 13, to describe religious reverence. In that case it is a plea not to apostasize, an exhortation in a day of peril and panic not to worship other gods to which many were turning, but quietly to reverence Jehovah and to take refuge in Him. This may well be Peter's meaning here, particularly if he wished, without more explicit mention, to refer to the pressure likely to be put on some Christians to join in Emperor worship or to revert to heathen idolatry (cf. iv. 3, 4). The following exhortation truly to reverence Christ 'as Lord' (RV), and not to hesitate, when asked, to confess their Christian hope, suits such a situation.

On the other hand, Is. viii. 12 may simply mean, 'Do not share their fear; do not join in the general panic' (cf. Pr. iv. 25). Certainly Peter here may mean (and the Greek can be so understood), 'Do not fear them; do not let them alarm you'. In that case the AV rightly conveys the sense. In either case there follows appropriately the further exhortation: *Neither be troubled.* The verb *tarassein* in the passive means 'to be disturbed'. It is used in Mt. ii. 3, xiv. 26; Jn. xiv. 1, 27.

15. In the Greek the reading 'Christ' instead of *God* is to be preferred. Language referring to Jehovah in Is. viii. 13 is explicitly applied to Jesus, thus claiming for Him, and particularly for Him as 'the Christ', *ton Christon*, the one who suffered, worship as God. Also, the order of the words in the Greek, beginning *Kurion de*, suggests that 'Lord' should be given predicative force. So RV gives the sense well: 'But sanctify in your hearts Christ as Lord.'

It is noteworthy that the sanctuary in which Christ is to be acknowledged as holy and worshipped is the heart. Such phraseology may have in mind circumstances due to persecution in which joining in corporate worship in the common meeting-place might be impossible. Christians are thus exhorted, whatever their circumstances, to enjoy living communion with Christ by realizing His indwelling Presence and by maintaining inner heart reverence towards Him. Such an exhortation also emphasizes the inner and spiritual character of all true Christian worship. It is ultimately independent of place. For Christ has promised to manifest His Presence, not in particular buildings, nor in connection with visible material objects, but with His people, in their hearts and in their midst (cf. Mt. xviii. 20, xxviii. 20).

Some think that the exhortation *be ready always to give an answer* implies the official persecution of Christians as Christians, and refers to the possibility of their having to face interrogation at a formal trial. *Be ready*, says the Greek, *pros apologian*, i.e. with a view to an apology, explanation, or speech in defence. Note the use of this word in Acts xxv. 16; 2 Tim. iv. 16, 'answer'; and in Phil. i. 16, 17, 'defence'. The accompanying phraseology in this verse, however, combines forcibly to suggest something which might be called for at any time in the most informal and spontaneous manner. The verb *aitein*, *asketh*, suggests ordinary conversation rather than an official enquiry. The words *always* and *to every man* make the reference completely general and comprehensive. The Christian must remember that anybody at any time may ask him to explain and justify his Christian confidence.

We have here some practical guidance concerning Christian witness. It is wrong to be always preaching at people. The Christian wife has been encouraged by Peter to seek to win her unbelieving husband without speaking to him on the subject (iii. 1). But the whole situation is changed if the other person asks for an explanation. Also, if Christians are on the alert, they may often rightly discern an implied question in some passing comment. Then is the time to speak; but one can do so only if one is seeking to be *ready*.

The Christian is then to engage, not in an aggressive attack on the other person's will or prejudice, but in a logical account (the word translated *reason* is *logos*), or reasoned explanation of the hope that is distinctive of the Christian community (cf. Heb. x. 23, RV). He ought, also, to do it *with meekness and fear*, i.e. without arrogance or self-assertion, with due respect and deference towards men, and with proper awe and reverence before God. For the spirit in which a statement is made may matter with some hearers more than its content. Only if they are attracted (or at least not put off) by the former will they give a proper hearing to the latter.

Many have understandably suggested that there may possibly be an implied allusion here to Peter's own failure when he denied the Lord. When he was unexpectedly asked by an unfamiliar person in an unusual place in a passing, superficial way he was not ready with his answer. And what he did say was spoken neither with meekness nor with reverence.

16. This verse is similar to ii. 12 and assimilation to its phraseology may be responsible for variations in the Greek MSS here. By conscientiously maintaining consistent good conduct Christians may, in the very matter in which they are slandered, put their detractors to shame by their virtuous behaviour. Christians can enjoy that liberty of spirit before God, which is indispensable to the effective giving of personal testimony to men, only if they maintain *a good conscience*. Indeed, to fail to do so is to endanger their own continuance in the faith (see 1 Tim. i. 19; Acts xxiv. 16). *En ho, whereas,* means literally 'in which' or 'in what', 'in the matter in relation to which', i.e. RV 'wherein' (cf. ii. 12). There is an alternative reading for the phrase *they speak evil of you* which is followed by RV. In it the same verb *katalalein*, 'to run down', 'to defame', occurs in the passive and in the second person plural, meaning 'ye are spoken against'. In the phrase *they may be ashamed,* RV 'put to shame', the compound Greek verb means 'shamed down', i.e. into silence, so as to be made to cease from reviling (cf. ii. 15; Lk. xiii. 17). The verb *epēreazein,* translated *falsely accuse,* means 'spitefully to abuse' (cf. Lk. vi. 28), 'despitefully (to) use'. For *conversation* RV has 'manner of life', which expresses the sense both of the Greek and of the AV English.

17. For should God so will, and He may, it is better to suffer as those doing good than to suffer as those who do evil. For when evil-doers suffer they are simply experiencing a consequence of their wrongdoing, something they deserve, an outworking of judgment, an expression in some measure of the divine sovereignty and of the moral character of the created order. But when well-doers suffer, their suffering is not a true moral consequence of their own well-doing, even though it may be their good actions that have provoked men thus to ill-treat them. Also, if the righteous God, who has established a moral order in creation, not only allows well-doers to suffer, but Himself wills that they should, it must be for some good reason and purpose. Far from such suffering being a penal consequence of their own evil-doing, in being thus ordered to happen to them, it must be intended to be a creative cause of good. God must intend that some profit or benefit should come out of it—for His own glory, for others' good, or the personal good of the sufferer himself. Such thinking brings Peter back in thought to the supreme example of such worthwhile suffering, the example from which he has himself been taught by Christ and the Spirit thus to think, namely, the suffering of the Christ who suffered at men's hands when Himself righteous, and for well-doing; and yet He suffered according to the will of God, and for the benefit of men.

VII. CHRIST'S SUFFERING AND ITS TRIUMPHANT CONSEQUENCES (iii. 18–22)

The suffering which Peter here has in mind is something unusual, something distinctively Christian. Its two surprising characteristics he has just explicitly defined (iii. 17). They are, on the one hand, that it should be undeserved (cf. ii. 19, 20), and, on the other, that it should be divinely ordained. Such suffering is distinctively Christian, first, because it is supremely illustrated in the suffering of Christ Himself and, second, because it is a pattern of experience in which His people are destined to share; for in thus suffering, He left us an example, that we should follow His steps (ii. 21).

In addition, as the prophets of Old Testament times were inspired of the Spirit to foresee (i. 10, 11), not only was such suffering foreordained for the righteous Christ; it was also His predestined road to glory. Once such suffering had befallen the Christ it was certain that corresponding glories would follow them. This meant that His human and once-for-all earthly sufferings were abundantly worth while; they were divinely and eternally rewarded. This is the particular theme to which Peter now returns and which he develops both here and in a later paragraph (iv. 12–19) in order to declare that such suffering, first, in the history of the Christ, and, second, in the history of His people, is of far-reaching heavenly consequence.

While Christ's sufferings and the sufferings of Christians are thus similar in principle and in outworking, Christ's sufferings were also unique both in character and in consequence. For when He suffered what He did not deserve, being Himself righteous, the suffering which He bore was the penalty due to the sins of the unrighteous, and in consequence of such suffering He achieved their reconciliation to God. Indeed, He thus suffered with this end in view that He might be able to bring sinners under judgment back to God.

Nor was His suffering unavailing. It issued in immediate and complete triumph and exaltation. Though He suffered the extreme penalty of sin for the unrighteous, and was personally put to death in the flesh, He was nevertheless quickened in the spirit. So He was at once able Himself to go and proclaim His triumph to the rebellious and imprisoned evil spirits, who had involved men in sin and judgment. He rose from the dead, and ascended into heaven. He is enthroned at God's right hand. All powers and authorities are made subject to Him. In other words, He is Lord of all, of death and life, of hell and heaven; and so He is able to save and to bring back to God those for whom He died.

These consequences of His sufferings and the benefits which they make possible are, therefore, intended to be entered into and enjoyed by us sinners. Christian baptism indicates the way of entrance, and seals upon our bodies the certain possibility of our full participation. A similar symbolical indication of God's way of salvation from judgment for sinners is found in the story of the ark and the flood. The ark passing safely through the flood provides a figure of God's method of saving men out of inevitable judgment. First, God delayed the day of judgment long enough for an ark to be prepared. Then, the souls that went into the ark did not avoid the judgment. Rather in the ark they were saved through the very water which drowned others, and, because of it, they thus passed out of the old world into a new world. When they emerged from the ark they literally found that old things had passed away, and all things were become new.

This figure is fulfilled in Christ (see, for example, 2 Cor. v. 17). He was prepared of God to come in the fulness of time. The judgment due to sin and sinners was meanwhile delayed. Then the judgment fell upon Him, as the flood waters upon the ark. When sinners take refuge in Him, they do not avoid the judgment due to sin, they are saved through its falling upon Christ; and, because of it, instead of meeting their own doom, are brought safe unto God.

Christian baptism directly corresponds as a figure of the way of salvation to the waters of the flood. For it witnesses to the proper judgment due to our sin, a judgment fulfilled in Christ's death for us. It indicates that if we are baptized into this death, i.e. Christ's death (cf. Rom. vi. 3, 4), we shall pass through and beyond the judgment due to sin, and emerge saved, free from condemnation, and sharers in Christ's risen life, on the farther side. This is how His suffering avails to bring us to God.

The hope of the benefit thus figuratively pledged being vitally realized in the sinner's experience is not to be found in any power in the baptism ceremony, or in the baptismal water, to wash away the filth of the flesh; but in a inward response of heart to God, and particularly in one's personal confession of faith in Christ crucified and risen. It is He, Christ incarnate, crucified, risen, enthroned, and not it, the baptism ceremony, who alone can make ours, as benefits of His passion, emancipation from sin and entrance into life. The striking theological phrases of this remarkable passage possibly reproduce almost *verbatim* some of the decisive statements used in the early Church when a convert to Christ confessed his faith at his baptism. Also, it seems more than probable that, when the truth of the gospel was preached on such occasions, the story of the ark and the flood was used as a significant scriptural illustration.

18. Peter reminds his readers again of Christ as the supreme example of the kind of suffering described in iii. 17. Such suffering was something which happened to Him and which He patiently endured. This recollection should make Christians view and face similar suffering differently. Christ suffered to the extreme limit of *being put to death in the flesh*. So 'suffered' here virtually means 'died', as it does in the so-called Nicene Creed: 'He suffered and was buried.' Some MSS do in fact read 'died' (see RV mg.).

For sins translates *peri hamartiōn.* This phrase in the singular is commonly used to describe a sin-offering, e.g. in LXX of Lv. v. 7, vi. 30 (cf. Rom. viii. 3; Heb. x. 6, 8). Since Christ Himself was sinless this kind of phraseology implies here that His suffering was atoning or propitiatory (cf. 1 Jn. ii. 2, iv. 10). It was also vicarious or substitutionary, *the just for the unjust.* It was the penalty due to the sins of the unrighteous that He bore in their stead, or the propitiation necessary for their sins that He offered on their behalf. This would give to them the status of those who cannot again be exposed to judgment for sins which have thus been punished, or for which propitiation has been already made (cf. Jn. v. 24; Rom. viii. 1). *Hapax, once,* means 'once for all'. Christ's sacrifice did not have to be repeated like the unavailing animal sacrifices of the Levitical ritual. The one event achieved a complete and final settlement of the issue raised by the sins of the unrighteous (cf. Heb. ix. 26, 28, x. 10–14).

Christ's suffering decisively removed the excluding barrier, and secured open access not only for Christ to come to God Himself, but also for Him to *bring us to God* (cf. Mk. xv. 38). This is the first and final goal of all religious activity, to secure reconciliation to God for sinners and the full, free, permanent enjoyment by them of unhindered access to God's presence and unbroken abiding in His company. The emphatic phrase which follows with its strong *put to death,* which suggests violence or execution, together with the previous word *suffered,* indicate the reality of Christ's physical suffering and death and the character of His end as a deliberate, painful termination of His earthly life, i.e. of 'the days of his flesh' (Heb. v. 7).

In the phrase *quickened by the Spirit* there is probably no reference to the Holy Spirit. *Flesh* and *spirit* are each without an article in the Greek and are best understood as references, in strong contrast, to two constituent parts or successive conditions of our Lord's human nature (cf. Mt. xxvi. 41; Rom. i. 3, 4; 1 Tim. iii. 16; see also 1 Cor. v. 5; 1 Pet. iv. 6). First we are told that His earthly life was abruptly terminated by penal execution, as though He were a sinner. Then, as a completely

unexpected 'anti-climax', we are told, not that His human
spirit went to Hades, there to await final judgment and the
second death, but that His human spirit enjoyed the benefit of
being *quickened*, i.e. it entered into fuller life (cf. Rom. i. 3, 4;
1 Cor. xv. 45). His physical death, therefore, was not the first
and earthly stage only of inevitable progress towards eternal
judgment (see Heb. ix. 27). Rather it was the point at which
the outworking of sin's judgment was once for all brought to a
head and terminated. His physical death was not a death in
sin, or under sin, but 'to sin', and to sin once and for all (see
Rom. vi. 10). He immediately began to enjoy liberation; He
was no longer straitened (Lk. xii. 50). Also, by such a physical
death He became not a victim but the Victor, the Lord over
death, and over all who, because of sin, were already victims
of death (see Rom. xiv. 9; Heb. II. 14, 15; Rev. i. 18). As in
the case of the rending of the veil of the temple immediately
His earthly life was ended (see Mk. xv. 37, 38), the phraseology
here stresses that positive benefits of His accomplished sacrifice,
or 'finished work', followed immediately upon His physical
death. His subsequent resurrection from the tomb was one of
these. But even before that happened He was already able to
move freely in the spiritual world as the victorious Man.

19. Christ was thus able at once to exercise, as Man, new
liberty and lordship. In His quickened human spirit, before
His body was raised from the tomb, He was able to go where
evil spirits are in prison, awaiting the judgment of the great
day (2 Pet. ii. 4, 5; Jude 6), and to announce to them His
victory over death, and over the consequences to men of their
evil-doing. He thus made them aware that their own judgment
was finally sealed (cf. Col. ii. 14, 15).

The verb *kērussein*, 'to herald' or 'proclaim' (see Rev. v. 2),
here translated *preached* is to be distinguished from *euangelizein*,
to proclaim good tidings (see especially iv. 6). Peter is not
saying that Christ preached the gospel. Rather He announced
His triumph over evil, which was for the evil spirits bad news.
Many have wished to interpret the phrase *the spirits in*

prison as a reference to departed human spirits; but it fits in with the linguistic usage of Scripture, and with the reference to the days of Noah, to understand it as a reference to fallen angels (cf. Gn. vi. 1–4; 2 Pet. ii. 4, 5). The word *pneumata*, *spirits*, alone and without qualification, is not thus used anywhere else in the Bible to describe departed human spirits. Note, for example, 'the spirits of just men' (Heb. xii. 23). But the word is thus used of supernatural beings, both good and bad (see Heb. i. 14; Lk. x. 20). To quote E. G. Selwyn, 'The facts that the word *pneumata* is used absolutely of supernatural beings, that Jewish tradition spoke of such beings . . . as disobeying God and transgressing their due order, and being punished by imprisonment, that the period of this transgression was always reckoned as immediately prior to the Flood; and that these beliefs are undoubtedly alluded to in 2 Pet. ii. and Jude 6, 7—these facts tell strongly in favour of this interpretation here.'[1]

20. *The longsuffering of God waited*, i.e. to give sinners time to repent, and to take refuge in the ark which was prepared, before the judgment fell (cf. Gn. vi. 3; Rom. ii. 4; 2 Pet. iii. 9). *Wherein* is *eis hēn*, 'into which', a phrase which suggests the activity of entering, *viz.*, 'by entering into which'.

The verb *diasōzein*, *saved*, means 'to bring safely through'. The preposition *dia* is repeated in *di' hudatos*, i.e. through water. So the sense may be that they were brought safely through the water (see RV mg.). Alternatively the preposition can signify *by* as in AV, or 'by means of', i.e. that the flood was the means of their salvation because the judgment which brought to others death paradoxically brought to them deliverance into a new world. This corresponds to the paradoxical truth of the gospel that by Christ's death sinners are not only themselves saved from death but brought into the enjoyment of new life. Also, as at the time of the flood this

---

[1] Most valuable, detailed examinations of the various problems and possibilities of interpretation in the understanding of this whole section of I Peter are to be found in Selwyn pp. 197–201; 314–362.

double benefit was enjoyed only by those who entered into the ark, so a similar double benefit is to be enjoyed under the gospel only by those who enter into Christ.

21. Baptism also is an antitype (the Greek is *antitupos*; cf. Heb. ix. 24), a corresponding *figure* of the way of salvation; but a richer and more direct figure, because it immediately relates those who are baptized to Jesus Christ and His death. Just as the flood spoke of a judgment, which those in the ark were both saved from, and saved by, in order to enjoy a new world, so the water of Christian baptism speaks of the death which fell upon Christ, a death due to sinners, which believers into Christ are both saved from, and saved by, and through which they enter into the enjoyment of new life before God. In the fulfilment of this pattern in the gospel it is *Christ's resurrection* which enables believers to share in this new life.

Here Peter deliberately adds two statements in parenthesis in order to make unmistakably plain that it is not mere participation in the outward form of baptism that saves. It is only Christ who can save through His death and resurrection, not the baptismal water and its administration. Those who would share in this salvation must enter into Christ crucified and risen. Such entrance and incorporation into Christ, though outwardly witnessed to and sealed by Christian baptism, are vitally realized by the individual only by the personal self-committal of faith into Christ and by genuine open confession of such faith to God, of which confession public baptism is normally the significant occasion.

The answer translates *eperōtēma*, 'demand', 'enquiry', 'interrogation'. This most probably refers to the questions and answers customary in baptism. There is evidence in papyri of the word being used for the formal question and consent which sealed a contract. It is possible to regard the parenthesis as ending with 'of a good conscience', and to connect the phrase *toward God* (*eis Theon*, 'unto God') directly with the main verb, i.e. 'baptism doth also now save us toward God'. It brings us safe to God. This corresponds with the purpose of

Christ's death expressed in iii. 18, to 'bring us to God'. It also
develops fully the positive issue of Christ's saving work and of
our initiation into Him. Not only are we saved from sin's
judgment, but we are also reconciled to God.

22. Here we have more of the victorious side of Christ's
suffering, a list of consequences which have followed His
death, and which demonstrate its value and His power fully
to save those for whom He died. It is as a Man that Christ has
been raised from the dead. His human body has been glorified.
He has gone into heaven. (The repetition of the Greek
participle *poreutheis*, which also occurs in iii. 19, suggests
successive stages in His triumphal progress.) He is enthroned
at God's right hand, the place of supreme privilege and
sovereignty in the universe. All the heavenly beings and
authorities are subject to His control. To confess all this at
baptism and in Christian worship, to be sure that the crucified
Jesus is alive, glorified and reigning, to acknowledge where He
now is (note the significant present tense, *Who . . . is on the right
hand of God*), was all part of true saving faith, the one all-
sufficient ground of the Church's existence and of Christians'
confidence and hope (cf. Rom. x. 9, 10; Eph. i. 19–22).

VIII. A FURTHER CALL TO HOLY LIVING (iv. 1–6)

These verses, like the preceding ones, contain statements
difficult of interpretation. In particular, we have to decide
what is meant by verses 1 and 6. Radically different interpretations of these verses are offered in the various commentaries. We do not intend, even in summary, to present all of
these. To do so might leave the reader confused rather than
helped. Here we deliberately follow, therefore, one line of
interpretation only, and seek to adhere to it in a way that may
give harmony to our understanding of the passage as a whole.
Put very briefly, what Peter says is that, because of Christ's
death for them, those who become Christians cannot live the

rest of their earthly lives as they did before; and, after death, which they still have to die, they will live eternally before God, and have no eternal judgment to face like other men.

Let us seek to appreciate in some detail the probable sequence of thought. In the opening phrase there is a reference back to Christ's suffering, which has been treated in the preceding verses, particularly iii. 18. That suffering was human and earthly, 'in the flesh', and meant in His case actually 'being put to death'. This is equally the sense in which it is in mind here. For being put to death, as He was, is the only form of 'suffering' that decisively brings a person's sinning to an end. Also in the sinless Christ's unique case, His death as the innocent substitute, who thus submitted to sin's penalty due to others, did finally terminate His relation to sin. When He thus died, He died unto sin once for all. Thenceforth He lives eternally as Man unto God (see Rom. vi. 10). Also, since the death which He thus died was for us (i.e. it was the penalty due to our sins), and since the benefit it procured of new life in fellowship with God is a benefit to be enjoyed by sinful men on whose behalf He thus suffered, these facts are meant decisively to alter both the way in which we live now, and the prospect before us beyond death. We ought, therefore, to face the future with a corresponding new attitude of mind.

In the first place, the intended result of Christ's death for us is that, for the rest of our earthly lives, we should spend our days differently, no longer just satisfying our selfish human appetites, but serving God's will; i.e. to use Paul's comparable phraseology, actively reckoning ourselves dead to sin but alive unto God, and consequently devoting our bodies to God in the service of righteousness (see Rom. vi. 11–13). For the days of our earthly lives which we spent in sin before we became Christians are days enough to have used in fulfilling heathen pleasures and joining in the common practices of carnal indulgence and in the unmentionable evils of idolatry. Henceforth we must renounce these old ways and live differently; and admittedly, if we do, our former companions in such evil-doings are bound to be surprised that we no longer share in their profligate excesses, and they may be expected to give expression to their displeasure by reviling us.

In the second place, particularly when we are reviled in this way, we must recognize the completely different position in which they and we stand in relation to God and to His inevitable judgment on evil-doers. For those who spend their earthly lives in indulgence and idolatry have yet to give an account to God. He will not fail in the coming day to judge all such men, whether they be then still alive or already dead. Beyond physical death there lies for them the prospect of eternal judgment (cf. Heb. ix. 27). How different is the state of Christians, even of those already dead, who have heard and embraced on earth the gospel of Christ's suffering for sins, the righteous for the unrighteous, to bring us to God. For them there is no coming day of judgment upon them as sinners. For them the judgment due to sin is completely a thing of the past. It has been settled and finished here on earth, in the flesh, by Christ's death. The last remaining earthly effect of it they tasted in their own physical death, when like other sinful men they died. But henceforth, according to God's purpose in the gospel, they permanently enjoy the positive benefit of Christ's death, that is new abiding spiritual life in fellowship with God.

1. The opening phrase, *Forasmuch then as Christ hath suffered for us in the flesh*, refers the readers back to iii. 18. It is a reminder that in His human body Christ not only endured pain; He was actually put to death. This brought to an end His relation to the sins of men, whose penalty He thus bore in His own body (ii. 24). He did not die 'in sin' or 'under sin' but 'to sin'. The new life which He was given as Man, when He was first 'quickened in the spirit' (iii. 18, RV), and then bodily raised from the dead, is a life henceforth wholly lived in devotion to God, and in the enjoyment of full and free access to His presence. Those for whose benefit He thus suffered are here challenged to arm themselves with a corresponding attitude of mind, and in consequence henceforth to spend life in a radically different fashion. They are challenged to appreciate that no-one can be properly initiated into Christ in baptism, and share in the benefits of His death and resurrection, without needing to recognize, first, that the consequence of having such a death reckoned as theirs must be to cease from sin, and second, that the intended purpose beyond it is that they should devote the rest of their earthly life, no longer to the indulgence of natural appetites, but wholly to the doing of God's will (cf. the similar teaching in ii. 24 and Rom. vi. 1–13).

Though omitted in some Greek MSS and in the RV, there is quite strong textual evidence to support the retention of the words *for us*. They certainly make explicit the unmistakable reference of the verse. For the substitutionary or vicarious character of Christ's sufferings is obviously in mind, and Christians are exhorted each for himself to share in their consequence and purpose, by reckoning himself dead to sin, and by letting his life henceforth be governed by the will of God. What is here inculcated is more than *imitatio Christi*, or the following of Christ's example. It is rather *unio mystica* or mystical union, a sense of dying with Christ to sin and of rising in Him to a new life which is to be lived for God. It is noteworthy, too, what importance is attached (both here and elsewhere in the New Testament) to a new and right attitude of mind as being fundamental to that radical change of behaviour which ought to express itself in the lives of all who belong to Christ (cf. Rom. xii. 2; Eph. iv. 17–24, especially 23).

Some would see in the words, *he that hath suffered in the flesh hath ceased from sin*, a reference to the purifying effect of physical suffering. So Archbishop Leighton (*in loc.*): 'Affliction sweetly and humbly carried doth purify and disengage the heart from sin, wean it from the world and the common ways of it.' But *ceased from sin* seems too strong and decisive a phrase thus to be interpreted. Also, consideration of the context and of similar exhortations in other Epistles suggests rather that Peter is here challenging Christians to enter into a consequence of Christ's suffering and not of their own suffering. Indeed, his teaching may be said to imply that, if only the Christian will actively reckon himself dead to sin and alive to God, he will not need the discipline of actual physical suffering or death to wean him from sin, or to bring the possibility of its continuance to an end (cf. 1 Tim. i. 20; 1 Cor. v. 5).

2. The striking statement of this verse indicates what is the ultimate purpose of Christ's suffering and what should be the proper response by Christians to its divine implications and intentions. It indicates the mind with which the Christian should arm himself to face life from now on. It indicates what should be the positive consequence of ceasing from sin. It indicates the principle or rule by which the rest of a Christian's earthly life should be governed, i.e. *the will of God*, not *the lusts of men*. In these two phrases two singular nouns stand in strong contrast to two plural ones. The Christian life, if rightly ordered, can enjoy a unity and an integration impossible to sinners. For there is only one true God; and for His people He has at any one time only one will. By contrast sinners are distracted and pulled first this way and then that by desire to satisfy the varied appetites which dominate those in whose company they find themselves.

3. Earthly life becomes divided for the Christian into *the time past*, before his conversion, and *the rest of his time in the flesh* (verse 2), after his conversion. He ought not to use any of the latter period still doing things characteristic of the former period. In those pre-conversion days life was spent not doing *the will of God* (verse 2), but working or executing (the verb is *kateirgasthai*, 'to carry into effect') *the will* (RV 'the desire'; Gk. *boulēma*, 'deliberate purpose', cf. Acts xxvii. 43) *of the Gentiles*, i.e. of godless men (cf. 1 Thes. iv. 5). What such activity involved is then explicitly and bluntly described, on the one hand, as forms of licentious physical indulgence, and on the other hand, as expressions of improper and misdirected religious worship. Peter's language implies (especially the perfect participle *peporeumenous*, 'having walked') that these are things which formerly his readers did actually share in, but now do so no longer (cf. 1 Cor. vi. 9–11).

Aselgeiai, lasciviousness, is a plural noun meaning 'excesses', 'open outrages against decency'. *Excess of wine* translates *oinophlugiai*, 'overflowings of wine', i.e. occasions of debauchery. *Potoi, banquetings*, means 'drinking parties'. *Athemitos, abominable*, means 'lawless' or 'unlawful', particularly acts violating the laws of nature and conscience, and so describes activity which stands condemned as improper even by human judgment.

4. These godless men *think it strange*, i.e. they are genuinely surprised, that those who have become Christians no longer keep them company in such excesses. *Excess of riot* means literally an overflowing or pouring out of prodigality or wastefulness. *Speaking evil of you* indicates one way in which Christians may find themselves reviled for their well-doing. Experience confirms that those who thus cease to keep company with their former friends in their indulgence and idolatry find that these very people sometimes begin quite unjustly to say malicious and slanderous things about them.

5. For *Who shall give account (logos)* cf. Mt. xii. 36, xviii. 23; Rom. xiv. 12; Heb. iv. 13. None can escape this final responsibility or answerability to God for the words and deeds of their earthly lives. *Ready to judge*, or according to some MSS 'judging readily', reminds us that it is of God's essential character to exercise judgment (cf. Jdg. xi. 27); and with His perfect knowledge He has all the necessary equipment to do it perfectly (cf. Gn. xviii. 25; Dt. xxxii. 4). *To judge the quick and the dead.* This brief comprehensive summary of God's certain future judgment of all men, no matter whether they be then still alive or already dead, occurs elsewhere in the New Testament (see Acts x. 42; 2 Tim. iv. 1), and later found its place in the creeds. Its normal reference in these places, and possibly therefore here also, is to a function to be discharged by Christ. God has appointed Him to be the Judge (see Jn. v. 22, 27; Acts xvii. 31; Rom. ii. 16). It is part of the full gospel or truth about God's purposes for men in Christ that Christ is appointed to deal with all the affairs of men, and particularly with their sin. Therefore those who do not receive Him as their Saviour,

must face Him as their Judge. Also, since He is God's appointed agent of judgment, His judgment is to be regarded as the judgment of God the Father.

6. The preaching of the gospel not only offers men the benefit of ceasing from sin and living differently for the rest of their earthly lives (iv. 1, 2); it also offers them the benefit of escaping judgment and entering into fuller spiritual life after death. Sin must be judged either here or hereafter. Sinners who do not respond to the gospel invitation must face judgment hereafter (iv. 5). But those who do respond find that the judgment due to sin is wholly completed here in the flesh, through the judgment which Christ bore for them. The last remaining sting of sin which they have to suffer is the death of their sinful and mortal earthly bodies. Beyond that lies spiritual quickening, and entrance into fuller life. This then is why the gospel was preached during their earthly lives to mortals who have since died physically. For when such people embrace the gospel, the judgment due to them as sinners is fully accomplished in this world, i.e. *in the flesh*; and *in the spirit*, both here and still more beyond death, they enter into life, and find themselves, through Christ's physical death and spiritual quickening, truly brought into God's presence (see iii. 18).

Some think it is possible to find here, and in iii. 19, an indication that an opportunity to hear the gospel is given to men after death. This interpretation is not clearly demanded by the actual statements; still less is it supported by their contexts. Nor does an idea of such far-reaching consequence find support elsewhere in the Bible. So we think it right to reject it. Not a few, including Augustine, Bede, Erasmus and Luther, have interpreted the statement as referring to the spiritually dead, to whom the gospel is preached in this world (cf. Jn. v. 25; Eph. ii. 1, 5, v. 14) that they may enter into spiritual life. Points against this second view are that the word *dead* has just been used in verse 5 of the physically dead; and the verb *was preached* is in the past tense. A point against the first view is that the preaching was done with a view to something happening to them while they were still *in the flesh*, or alive on earth; it cannot, therefore, have taken place after death.

We definitely prefer, therefore, the third view given above that during their earthly lives the gospel was preached even to those who have since died, in order that the judgment due to them as human sinners might be decisively accomplished here and now in the flesh, and that they might eternally enjoy a spiritual life like God's, as partakers of the divine nature. (In the Greek there is a significant contrast between the aorist tense of *judged* and the present continuous *live*.)

Thus the tables will be turned. Whereas those whose lives here in the flesh are governed by the lusts of men will after death face judgment, those who here and now embrace the gospel not only pass in this life beyond the judgment due to sin but also begin to enjoy new spiritual life which abides beyond death and qualifies for fellowship with God (cf. Jn. v. 24).

IX. THE PRACTICAL DEMANDS OF CHRISTIAN DISCIPLESHIP (iv. 7–11)

This paragraph concludes the second main section of the Epistle. It provides us with a brief, positive indication of the practical demands of Christian discipleship. (i) Christian life should be lived in the light of the impending consummation. (ii) Christians ought, therefore, to keep their heads, and not be carried away by self-indulgence or excitement. (iii) They ought to preserve the mental alertness necessary to sustained and effective praying. (iv) They ought to give priority to the active expression of love for one another, particularly by being ready to show hospitality. (v) They should show faithfulness in stewardship by exercising in ministry to one another their God-given gifts, whether in word or deed. (vi) They should thus seek in everything to glorify God through Jesus Christ.

7. Christian believers know that the Christ, who has come to suffer and to save, is to be God's agent in the judgment of men. Peter has just referred (iv. 5) to 'him that is ready to judge the quick and the dead'. They should also know that the true fulfilment of their calling and destiny in Christ lies beyond death and the present world-order, in a 'salvation ready to be revealed in the last time' (i. 5), at 'the appearing of Jesus Christ' (i. 7). This earthly life in the flesh, and this present age are not to go on for ever. There are to be both a termination and a consummation of *all things*. Also, this inevitable *end is at hand*. It is always to be thought of as impending. This awareness should disturb their complacency, and make them face daily living with a new sense of eternal values. It provides a further reason for abandoning a life of self-indulgence, and for practising self-discipline, prayer, and loving service of the brethren. In this emphasis on the coming consummation and its consequent practical challenge we may trace the influence of the teaching of our Lord Himself. He had spoken, on the one hand, of similarity to the days of Noah (cf. iii. 20), and of men and women wholly occupied with passing worldly interests (cf. iv. 3, 4), until the judgment of the flood came and overwhelmed them all (see Lk. xvii. 26, 27). He had spoken, on the other hand, of the responsibility of stewards to be found both watchful and active in faithful service at their Lord's appearing (Lk. xii. 35-43).

Be ye therefore sober, or 'of sound mind' (RV). The verb *sōphronein*, 'to be in one's right mind', 'in control of oneself', is used to describe the restored demoniac at Gadàra (Mk. v. 15). It is also used in contrast both to being 'beside oneself' or 'mad' (2 Cor. v. 13), and to 'thinking too highly of oneself' (Rom. xii. 3). There are dangers to spiritual well-being in intemperance, uncontrolled excitement or frenzy, and conceit. This sinful and self-indulgent world is not the place to lose one's mental or moral balance. Those who would be ready for Christ's appearing must keep their head and conscience clear.

Watch unto prayer, or 'be sober unto prayers' (RV and RV mg.), enforces the same exhortation for the added reason that such sobriety is indispensable to full prayerfulness. Christians must not allow their minds to become fuddled or dazed by drink or drowsiness. They should keep themselves awake and alert, with all their faculties under control, in order to be able to give themselves to praying. Peter possibly had in mind here the way in which in the garden of Gethsemane he failed to pray because he went to sleep and failed to watch. As a result, he was unprepared to withstand temptation (see Mk. xiv. 37–40, 66–72).

8. The presence of active mutual love among Christians is assumed. The exhortation in this verse is to its pre-eminence and its strenuous maintenance. *Fervent, ektenēs,* does not refer to warmth of emotion, but, as Cranfield puts it, to the 'taut muscle of strenuous and sustained effort as of an athlete'. The root idea is 'stretched' or 'strained'. The verb 'to stretch out' is used by Xenophon to describe a horse made to go at full gallop. So the adjective suggests intensity, earnestness, exerting one's powers to their full extent. Such practice of love for one another matters more than everything else among Christians. Love is the comprehensive virtue that should complete and crown all other activity (cf. Col. iii. 14). It ought to be treated as the priority in Christian living. Its practice among Christians is the chief way in which they are to show themselves different from others, truly children of God and disciples of Christ (see 1 Jn. iii. 14, iv. 7, 8; Jn. xiii. 34, 35).

Peter proceeds to indicate explicitly the way in which love works and should work among Christian brethren. It *covers the multitude of sins.* It is ready to forgive again and again. It finds a way to shelter the wrongdoer from exposure and condemnation. This is how God has treated us. This, therefore, is how we ought to treat one another. Similar words are to be found in Pr. x. 12: 'Hatred stirreth up strifes: but love covereth all sins.' There the meaning plainly is that love refuses to see faults (cf. 'Love thinketh no evil', 1 Cor. xiii. 5). It would seem to be in this sense that Peter quotes the words here. By later Christian writers (e.g. Tertullian and Origen) the words are interpreted as indicating that by showing love to others a man covers his own sins. This does not, however, necessarily imply the idea that one can win forgiveness by showing kindness. It is much more likely to have been inspired by our Lord's reiterated teaching that only those who forgive others may expect to continue to enjoy God's forgiveness (see Mt. vi. 14, 15; Mk. xi. 25, 26).

9. Another way in which Christian love may find active practical expression is in showing *hospitality* to Christians from other places, who as strangers or visitors are personally unknown, but who need shelter and food. By becoming Christians many ceased to enjoy the welcome and help of former potential friends. They stood, therefore, in urgent need of compensating Christian friendship at the hands of those who were now their brethren in Christ. Similarly, Christian missionaries, who left their home churches and lifelong friends, and travelled here and there to make the gospel known, often needed material support and help on their way from the Christian brethren whose churches they might visit. Without it the continuance of their work would have been impossible. So such injunctions to hospitality are frequent. See Rom. xii. 13 ('pursuing hospitality', RV and RV mg., i.e. keeping at it); 1 Tim. iii. 2; 3 Jn. 5-8.

The insertion of the phrase *without grudging*, RV 'murmuring', implies that the demands on some of showing such hospitality were frequent and heavy, and that naturally they might have been tempted to be resentful and complaining. But such opportunities of showing love to Christian brethren in need ought to be gladly embraced as a Christian privilege, and indeed a form of service to Christ Himself (see Mt. xxv. 35, 38, 40). Also, such ministry can be undertaken in the confidence that God will provide all that is needful, and that such service will bring its own surprising rewards (see 2 Cor. ix. 6-8; Heb. xiii. 2).

10. It is implied here that every Christian has received some *gift* from God, a gift which is to be held in trust for the benefit of the whole Church, and to be exercised in ministry for the good of others. The ministry of each is to be according to the character of his particular gift, and this is primarily determined not by men but by God (cf. 1 Cor. xii. 4–11). These gifts differ widely; but they are all alike God-given manifestations of the very varied (*poikilos*, lit. 'variegated') *grace of God*. God thus equips each one of His family or household for service, and makes him responsible as a *steward* to use his endowment in the service of his brethren. Such equipment for service is not, therefore, to be thought of as restricted to a privileged minority in the Church, i.e. the special ministers. Every Christian may expect particular divine endowment for some form of ministry, and he should recognize his corresponding responsibility before God as a steward for its proper use. Also, the members of the Christian community are thereby made by God interdependent. No one Christian believer can fully enjoy the benefits of the grace of God in Christ, or fully express the new activities it makes possible, in isolation. For Christians can receive essential help, and themselves fulfil their individual calling to service, only in active intercourse together. The verb *diakonein*, 'to minister', or 'serve', is a very general word, and can embrace all kinds of service rendered to others. For example, in Acts vi. 1–4 the verb and the corresponding noun, *diakonia*, are used both of 'serving tables' (i.e. distributing food) and of the ministry of the word.

11. Two main types of Christian ministry to the brethren are distinguished in this verse: first, ministry by the spoken word, i.e. preaching, teaching, etc.; secondly, ministry in deeds, in acts of practical kindness, such as showing hospitality. The phrase *if any man speak* would seem to cover here all forms of ministry by word of mouth. *Oracles*, *logia*, is elsewhere used to refer to the Scriptures, or to words from God's mouth (see Rom. iii. 2; Acts vii. 38). Some wish here to treat *logia* as nominative, and to interpret the phrase as meaning, 'as the Scriptures speak', i.e. with truth and sincerity, taking the Bible for his model. While this is possible, it seems more likely that *logia* is meant as an accusative, conveying the sense, 'Let what he says be as words spoken by God Himself'.

Deeds of practical kindness are probably implied in the phrase, *if any man minister.* These, too, are a form of ministry or divine service. That with which it is discharged, e.g. money, is therefore to be regarded as a divine gift involving a stewardship. The need for this awareness applies equally to every kind of personal possession with which ministry to others can be discharged, whether it be material resources, natural aptitude, or physical strength. For *the ability which God giveth,* RV has 'the strength which God supplieth'. The verb *chorēgein,* 'to supply', carries with it the sense of 'to equip', 'to furnish for the public good'. Proper awareness of the divine source and of the abundant supply of such ability demands that the service which it makes possible should be rendered modestly and strenuously, acknowledging God's enabling, and using it to the full.

That God in all things may be glorified is the intended goal and the crowning satisfaction of Christian service. God is thus glorified when the variety and value of the gifts of His grace are openly manifested in their diligent exercise, and when the ministry thus accomplished is plainly due to God's enabling. *To whom be praise and dominion* is better read, as in RV, as a statement, not a prayer, 'whose is the glory and the dominion'. The *Amen* is then a form of endorsement, 'So it is', rather than of request, 'So be it'. Also, while this statement might refer to God, in the context here and in the light of similar statements elsewhere (see 2 Tim. iv. 18; 2 Pet. iii. 18; Rev. i. 6), it is best understood as referring to Jesus Christ.

X. FURTHER TEACHING ABOUT CHRISTIAN SUFFERING (iv. 12-19)

Trial and suffering, endured because of our Christian faith, should be regarded not with surprise or shame, but with rejoicing and as a means of glorifying God. For they are no strange mischance, interfering with the fulfilment of God's purpose. Rather they are the divinely-appointed way of testing and purifying faith. God can and does use them to further His own ends. Also, they are to be viewed as a sharing in Christ's sufferings, an experience which makes us, or proves that we are, peculiarly one with Him. Such a privilege is in itself cause for rejoicing, the more so because it holds sure promise of an overwhelmingly joyful participation in Christ's coming manifested glory. And those who now share Christ's reproach at the hands of men, share also in the crowning blessing granted to God's true temple, that is, participation in that manifested glory of the divine Presence which is made ours by the indwelling Spirit.

The distinctive experience, which is thus to be reckoned and proved to be a blessing, is to be reproached for the name of Christ, as a Christian. We must make sure, therefore, that any suffering which we experience is genuinely Christian and undeserved. For there is no joy or glory in suffering as an evil-doer, or in bringing trouble upon oneself by unwarranted interference in other people's lives.

These sufferings of Christians are the initial stages of God's judgment of sinful men. They are purificatory with a view to salvation, though they involve temporary earthly pain and loss. The final stages of God's judgment will bring only condemnation and eternal loss on the ungodly who obey not the gospel of God. So, those who know that their sufferings are according to God's will, and not a result of their own evil-doing, should keep up their well-doing, trusting that God, even through the suffering, will deal with them faithfully for their eternal good, and bring them in the end with Christ to glory.

12. *Beloved.* The introduction of this address to the readers marks the beginning of the third and final main division of the Epistle (cf. ii. 11). It is interesting that Peter's address on the day of Pentecost similarly divides into three sections, each of which is introduced by a fresh use of the vocative (see Acts ii. 14, 22, 29). The idea of *purōsis, fiery trial* (lit. 'burning'), is that of 'trial by fire', a process used in the refining of metals. Cf. i. 7, where there is explicit mention of testing gold by fire. The idea is to be found in Pr. xxvii. 21 (where the LXX uses a similar vocabulary): 'The fining pot is for silver, and the furnace for gold' (RV; cf. Ps. lxvi. 10; Rev. iii. 18). *Think it not strange*, i.e. do not be surprised or astonished by its strangeness or unexpected character. For it 'cometh upon you to prove you' (RV), i.e. it is something whose happening to you has been directly ordered of God for an explicit purpose, *viz.*, for a test or trial to prove character and quality. It has been aptly suggested that Gentile converts to Christ, as distinct from Jewish believers, would be particularly unused to persecution on account of their religion. Naturally, therefore, they would regard suffering consequent upon becoming Christians as a strange misfortune, wholly out of place, something which contradicted the promised blessings of the gospel.

13. By contrast the Christian attitude to suffering should be completely different. According as their sufferings are a participation in the sufferings appointed for, and associated with, God's Christ, they ought not to be astonished or resentful, but to rejoice, and to go on rejoicing. (The verb *chairete* is present tense, demanding not a single isolated response, but a continuous attitude and activity.) For it means that they have a privileged share in the outworking of God's age-long purpose, according to which His Christ enters His glory, through suffering (cf. i. 10, 11; Lk. xxiv. 26). To share, therefore, in Christ's sufferings here, is to be on the sure road to a share in His consequent glory hereafter (cf. Mt. v. 11, 12; Heb. xi. 26). And not only in this life is there ground for continuous rejoicing. When Christ's destined glory is openly manifest, when the whole universe sees and acknowledges Him as Lord, there will be a much greater outburst of joyful exultation. So to suffer with rejoicing now is the way to prepare to rejoice with exultation then (cf. i. 7; Rom. viii. 17, 18; 2 Thes. i. 4–7; Tit. ii. 11–13). The prospect of such rapturous joy then should also be a compelling reason for continuing to rejoice now—while still in the midst of tribulation (cf. Rom. v. 2, 3, xii. 12).

14. *If ye be reproached for the name of Christ, happy are ye* states the paradoxical truth of present Christian experience, namely, that to have to suffer reproach for Christ's sake is not a misfortune to be resented in self-pity but a privilege for which to thank God and to congratulate oneself (cf. Acts v. 41). The words clearly re-echo the teaching of our Lord Himself (see Mt. v. 11). This reproach comes through acknowledging Jesus and being associated with Him as the promised Messiah or Christ of God, the Lord's anointed. All who would show loyalty to Him, and share in ministry to His redeemed people, are always liable to have to share in this reproach. It is part of their earthly calling (cf. Pss. lxix. 7–9, lxxxviii. 50, 51; Heb. xi. 26, xiii. 13).

For the spirit of glory and of God resteth upon you. Jesus was sealed from above as God's Christ—He was anointed—by the coming to rest upon Him of the Spirit of the Lord (see Jn. i. 29–34; cf Is. xi. 2, lxi. 1). So His people, who bear His reproach and suffer for His Name, are owned as His by a special anointing or manifestation of the Spirit of God. Similarly in Old Testament times the tabernacle or temple was marked as God's dwelling place by the coming of the *shekinah* or 'glory' of the Lord, symbolically visible as a pillar of cloud or fire (see Ex. xxxiii. 9, 10, xl. 34, 35). It is such special manifestation by God of His Presence with His people of which the persecuted are here assured (cf. Jn. xiv. 23).

The actual phraseology is variously interpreted. It is possible to regard 'the glory' (the Greek has the definite article) as a personal reference to the Son, as 'the glory' of the Godhead. (For other places where a similar interpretation is possible, see 2 Cor. iii. 18, iv. 6; Jas. ii. 1.) Thus understood this verse provides a striking reference to the three Persons of the Trinity, and indicates that the Spirit who comes to dwell in Christians' hearts is the Spirit of Christ as well as the Spirit of God.

Others treat the phrase, *tō tēs doxēs,* lit. 'the of the glory' (to make sense some accompanying noun such as 'spirit' must be understood) as a reference to something other than the Spirit. For instance, it is possible to supply 'name', particularly as it has occurred in the previous sentence. The holy city, and particularly, the temple, was described as the place where God put His name (see 1 Ki. viii. 29, ix. 3, xiv. 21). Or the phrase may virtually mean 'the manifestation of the glory', i.e. the *shekinah.* Or it may mean that the very suffering itself is a kind of hall-mark of the glory. For those who share in Christ's suffering here and now are thereby assured of a share in His coming glory.

The sentence beginning *on their part . . .* is omitted in RV. It does not seem to have been part of the original text of the Epistle. It may be an explanatory comment, possibly added very early in some MS, explaining the paradox of Christians' glorifying Christ by faithfully enduring, for His sake and as His confessed followers, blasphemous reproaches directed at His name.

15. When the people of God endure undeserved suffering for Christ's sake, they experience fellowship with Him and bring glory to His name. It is doubly important, therefore, that they should not bring justly deserved suffering upon themselves either by evil-doing or by indiscreet action. For not only are such practices wrong in themselves; but also, when professing Christians thus clearly deserve punishment, the distinctive witness of true Christian suffering is undermined and contradicted.

Paschein, suffer, is too general a word to justify the assertion that legal punishment at the hands of the civil or imperial authorities is what is unmistakably in mind, though reference to it may well be included, particularly in regard to offences such as murder or theft. The necessity to warn Christians against committing such crimes as these is some indication of the character of the social environment, and the previous history and habits of these converts to Christianity. They needed awakening to the truth that such things could now be done by them no more (cf. 1 Cor. vi. 9-11; Eph. iv. 28, v. 3-12).

A busybody (RV 'a meddler') *in other men's matters* translates *allotrioepiskopos,* a supervisor of things not one's own or belonging to another. Note that *hōs, as,* occurs before *murderer* and again before *busybody,* but not before *thief* or *evildoer.* Its repetition here suggests that a different class is being mentioned. The previous three are all forms of wrongdoing capable of being committed by Christian and non-Christian alike. This activity is something peculiar to Christians with which they only might be charged and have to suffer. Some think there is a reference here to the possible legal accusation and punishment of Christians as responsible for causing family and commercial discord and disturbance (cf. Mt. x. 35, 36; Acts xvi. 19, xix. 24-27). It seems much more likely to be a reference to possible ill-treatment in which Christians might become involved at the hands of their neighbours as a consequence of unwise and improper interference in other people's lives. For while it is imperative for the Christian to begin to order his own conduct according to new standards of purity and justice, this new awareness and concern does not qualify him officiously to interfere in the lives of others, particularly non-Christians, to try to make them live according to his light.

16. The name *Christian* was first given to believers in Jesus as a nickname by Gentile onlookers, who seem to have realized that here was a religious movement distinct from Judaism (see Acts xi. 26). The name was used by Agrippa in scorn (see Acts xxvi. 28). It is its unfriendly use that is clearly here in mind. Obviously, in some circumstances, the very fact of thus being known *as a Christian* was enough to bring upon the bearer of such a name social obloquy or ostracism or possibly official persecution. What Peter asserts is that there is no cause for shame in having to suffer on this account, or in being so called. Rather does such open recognition by others give the Christian opportunity to glorify God by the way in which he lives up to it. *On this behalf* translates *en tō merei toutō*, 'in this respect'. RV, following an alternative and preferable reading, renders 'in this name', i.e. because he is so called (cf. iv. 14).

17, 18. Peter now adds a complementary truth concerning the present earthly sufferings of God's people. This, he says, is the season for God's judgment to begin from His own household, i.e. from us Christians. In its consummation it will be manifested against unbelievers, those who *obey not*, or knowingly reject, *the gospel of God*, and refuse to believe it. The doom, therefore, that awaits them is terrible to contemplate. For if God, the righteous Judge, so hates evil, and must deal with it, that He judges His redeemed people, what will be the fate of unbelievers, when His full wrath against sinners is revealed? Or, if the justified sinner who is seeking to do God's will is saved only with difficulty, because through judgment, and with inevitable pain and loss, what will be the end of the ungodly and sinful, who is doubly wrong, both in his heart attitude to God and in the evil practices of his life? Verse 18 quotes the LXX version of Pr. xi. 31.

There is here a further comparison of Christians to the sanctuary or temple where God manifests His presence (cf. iv. 14). While God's coming to possess His people is assured, it cannot be realized without preparatory judgment and purification. Prophetic indication of this prior necessity is given in Ezk. ix (see especially verse 6) and Mal. iii. 1–6, 17, 18, iv. 1. The same prophets also make plain that, after God has thus delivered His people by judgment, and made them fit for His presence, He will deal with sinners in judgment to destroy them from before His face, to banish them to outer darkness, to give them no more standing in His sight. So, Peter asks, where shall such appear? (Cf. 2 Thes. i. 4–10.)

Peter thus repeats with a new emphasis truths stressed before, namely, that those who share in God's judgment on sin here will find salvation hereafter, whereas those who live here in ungodliness and sin must face terrifying final judgment hereafter. While there are brevity and reserve in what he says, it at least suggests that, in so far as those who become Christians need purgatorial cleansing before they can share the heavenly glory, it is meted out to them, not in some intermediate state, but in this life. If God in His providence permits them to be disciplined by such suffering, it is in order that their spirits may be saved in the day of Christ (cf. iv. 6; 1 Cor. v. 5). Such an understanding of iv. 17, 18 possibly throws some additional light on the intended significance of the reference to judgment in the flesh in iv. 6.

19. Christians need to recognize, therefore, that for more than one reason the experience of suffering in this life may be for them *according to the will of God*. It may be God's way to bring them into a fuller share either of Christ's glory or of His own holiness (cf. Rom. viii. 17, Heb. xii 5 11). As the *Creator*, or orderer of life, God is *faithful*, and may be counted on to fulfil His declared plan and purpose. There is every reason, therefore, why Christians should with confidence commit their souls to God's care even when they suffer. In addition they should make their own contribution to the furtherance of His will and the promotion of His glory in the world by themselves sustaining active well-doing. They should not allow themselves to be put off doing this by resentment either against God for His harsh providence or against men for their hard treatment. Rather they should learn from Christ's example and follow His steps (ii. 21). For, when He suffered, He did not retaliate with evil either in deed or word; rather He committed Himself in quiet confidence to God, the righteous Judge (ii. 22–24; cf. Lk. xxiii. 46; Ps. xxxi. 5). It seems possible that our Lord's actual final prayer before His death on the cross was here in Peter's mind.

XI. THE RESPONSIBILITIES OF ELDERS (v. 1–4)

Peter here addresses those responsible in the local churches for the pastoral care of God's flock. He identifies himself with them as 'a fellow-elder'. His special claim to a responsive hearing is based on his unique personal experience as a witness of Christ's earthly suffering and heavenly glory. He exhorts them to be devoted and zealous in the discharge of their task, to lead by example rather than to try to drive by domineering self-assertion. The proper discharge of pastoral care or over-sight in the Church of God includes, as the phraseology of verses 2–4 suggests, provision and protection, supervision and discipline, instruction and direction. The detailed indication of the way in which elders should perform such ministry mentions six points in three pairs, each containing a negative and a positive injunction. Their work should be done: (i) for the right reason, or in the right spirit, not because they must, but because they freely choose so to do; (ii) with the right motive, not for material gain, but for the sheer delight of doing it, i.e. finding satisfaction in the job itself rather than in what they get out of it; (iii) in the right manner, not driving but leading, not domineering but setting an example. To this is added a promise, which implies that such work should also be done (iv) with a proper awareness that in it they serve the chief Shepherd to whom they are answerable; and that He will Himself reward service rendered with rewards that are eternal.

1. The RV (rendering the preferable Greek reading, *oun*) includes 'therefore' in the opening phrase. This suggests that the exhortation takes its rise from the previous section concerning inevitable trials and judgment. The connecting thought possibly is that elders, as the most privileged and most responsible members of the house of God, are the most exposed to God's judgment. The highest standard of all is expected of them (cf. Ezk. viii. 11, 12, ix. 5, 6, especially 'then they began at the ancient men'; Mal. iii. 2, 3, especially 'he shall purify the sons of Levi'; see also Jas. iii. 1). Or possibly the idea is that the inevitability of earthly trials and of divine judgment in the experience of God's people makes all the more urgent the need for faithfulness in pastoral care.

The title *elders, presbuteroi*, 'presbyters', describes their status as seniors or leaders. 'Bishops' (*episkopoi*, 'overseers') and 'pastors' (*poimēnes*, 'shepherds') seem in the early Church of the New Testament times to have been alternative names for those here called 'elders'. These other two names indicate the character of the elders' ministry or responsibility. This connection Peter here explicitly confirms (in verse 2) by his exhortation of elders concerning feeding or tending the flock (*poimainein*, 'to act as shepherds') and taking or exercising the oversight (*episkopein*, 'to oversee', or 'to act as bishops'). Although the English word 'priest' is etymologically derived from 'presbyter'—it is 'presbyter' writ short—it is confusing rather than helpful to use 'priest' to translate the Greek *presbuteros*. For 'priest' has become the accepted word, and the only current word, to translate the Greek *hiereus*, one who offers sacrifice, and ministers Godward (see Heb. v. 1). This is an entirely different kind of ministry, and one never explicitly or exclusively ascribed in the New Testament to presbyters, but rather to the whole people of God. Hence the phrase 'the priesthood of the laity' (cf. ii. 5). The lack here of the definite article before *presbuteroi* and the use of the same word in verse 5 to describe those older over against those younger possibly implies a wide reference, including all senior members of local congregations, who in any way exercise pastoral care over others.

For *who am also an elder*, RV has 'who am a fellow-elder' (Gk. *sumpresbuteros*). Peter does not give orders as an apostle, but with sympathetic fellow-feeling, as one called to similar responsibility to theirs, he encourages and urges them in devotion to duty. In thus speaking he is obeying his own injunction (see verse 3) not to lord it over fellow Christians, but to set them an example and to serve them in humility. *Martus, a witness*, means strictly not a spectator, but a giver of testimony. Obviously only the person who has been the one can fully be the other (see Jn. xv. 27; Acts i. 21, 22). So Peter's consciousness of his special privilege as an eyewitness of *the sufferings of Christ* may rightly be associated here with his confessed awareness of a personal responsibility, put upon him by the risen Lord, to be a witness 'of these things', i.e. to give testimony about them (see Lk. xxiv. 44–48; cf. Acts i. 8). *The glory that shall be revealed* is the glory divinely destined for God's Christ (i. 11), a glory given to Christ after His resurrection (i. 21), a glory yet to be openly revealed (cf. iv. 13), and a glory in which Christ's people, including Peter, are then to share as joint-heirs with Him (see Rom. viii. 17, 18). Peter's description here of himself as *a partaker* or sharer in it, however, may rather be a reference to the special privilege granted to him when he saw Jesus transfigured (cf. 2 Pet. i. 16, 17). The transfiguration of our Lord is thus regarded as a preview of Christ's glory as it will be manifested at His appearing or second coming (see verse 4).

2. In urging the elders to *feed the flock of God which is among you* Peter is giving to others the very same command which he was himself given by the risen Lord (see Jn. xxi. 16). The verb *poimainein* includes all that is involved in the shepherd's task in looking after the flock. These shepherds are reminded that the flock is God's, not theirs, and that they are only under-shepherds (cf. Ps. c. 3; Ezk. xxxiv. 7–10). Also, God has only one flock. It is portioned out among the shepherds, each of whom has a charge allotted to him (see verse 3, RV) in relation to which he is to fulfil his ministry. *Not by constraint* means not of necessity or under a sense of compulsion (cf. 2 Cor. ix. 7). After the words *but willingly* (i.e. 'voluntarily') some MSS add *kata Theon*, RV 'according unto God', i.e. in accordance with His purpose, freely choosing to do what they know to be God's will. Alternatively, it may mean 'after the pattern of God', i.e. following or copying Him (cf. Lk. vi. 36). *Not for filthy lucre* means not moved by desire for base or sordid gain. This seems to imply that such ministers received remuneration—which is not here forbidden—and that such ministry was engaged in by some simply as a means of obtaining material advantage (cf. 1 Tim. v. 17; Tit. i. 11).

3. For *over God's heritage*, RV has 'over the charge allotted to you'. The Greek, *hoi klēroi*, seems here to mean your respective

allotments or portions. *Being ensamples* translates *tupoi gino-
menoi*, the force of which is 'becoming models', i.e. showing
yourself as patterns to be copied by the flock.

4. The use of *phanerōthentos*, *shall appear*, RV 'be manifested',
suggests that a time is coming when all will see Christ. Meanwhile Christian pastors should do their work as already seeing
Him, and seen by Him, and having due regard for the recom-
pense of the reward (cf. Heb. xi. 26, 27). He is the one 'Arch-
shepherd' (the Greek is *archipoimenos*) or Archbishop, to whom
the under-shepherds are answerable and by whom they will be
rewarded.

A crown was in the world of that day the reward for victorious
achievement, e.g. in the games (see I Cor. ix. 24, 25). The
phrase *a crown of glory* means not just 'a glorious crown', but a
share in glory as one's reward (cf. 'a crown of life', Jas. i. 12;
Rev. ii. 10). *That fadeth not away* translates *amarantinos*, an
adjective meaning 'made of amaranth', a flower which was
supposed never to fade, and so to be 'everlasting' (cf. i. 4).

XII. AN EXHORTATION TO HUMILITY AND
ENDURANCE (v. 5-9)

It is similarly important that all Christians should seek to
adopt a right attitude of mind and response of spirit in relation
to their fellows and their circumstances. They should act in
ready submission and willing service, particularly in relation
to their elders, and above all in relation to God Himself. They
should be both restrained and inspired by the awareness that
God sets Himself against the self-assertive, but that He
sustains, and, in due time, will exalt the submissive. He can be
confided in because He cares. All anxiety should, therefore, be
cast upon Him. At the same time, self-control and watchful-
ness must be maintained. For the devil is an active and an
aggressive foe, out to destroy Christian faith and testimony.
He is, therefore, to be resisted by a steadfast persistence in
such faith and testimony, a persistence that will be helped by

not forgetting that the suffering for Christ's sake in which they may consequently be involved, is no unusual or unique experience, but demands an endurance which is part of God's foreordained purpose for His people in this world.

5. The word *likewise* seems simply to introduce another similar exhortation to worthy conduct (cf. iii. 1). Peter repeatedly stresses the practice of willing subjection and submission in giving others honour and doing them service (cf. ii. 13, 18, iii. 1). Such active practice of humility becomes every member of the Christian family, particularly the *younger*, who are easily tempted to unhealthy self-assertion. *The elder, presbuteroi*, probably refers not exclusively to those given a status as overseers, but to all who are senior in years.

The unusual verb *egkombousthai*, translated *be clothed*, describes putting on a garment which was tied on over others with a knot, e.g. an apron. The sense is 'gird on humility as an apron'. Such phraseology, particularly when thus used by Peter, vividly recalls the upper room, where Peter saw Jesus gird Himself in this way and stoop to wash His disciples' feet. *Humility, tapeinophrosunē*, i.e. 'lowliness of mind', is fundamentally an attitude of mind. The exhortation here is not to feel humble, nor to pray for humility, but to act it, to give humility expression in serving others, in taking orders from them, and in fitting into their arrangements. The RV adds 'to serve one another', and omits *be subject one to another*. This seems a preferable rendering of the probable original Greek. *Allēlois* simply means 'towards one another', i.e. for each other's good.

The words *for God resisteth the proud, and giveth grace to the humble* are quoted from Pr. iii. 34 (cf. Pss. xviii. 25, 26, cxxxviii. 6; Lk. i. 51–53). All men do well to remember that God watches how they act and treats them accordingly. The haughty or arrogant He sets Himself against. To the lowly He grants favour. They find acceptance in His sight, and in the sight of men (see Gn. xxxix. 21). They enjoy bounty at His hands. He sustains them.

6, 7. Here both the highest direction and wider range are given to the governing principle of willing and active submission. Such deliberate self-subjection ought to be practised by Christians primarily towards God Himself—they should humble themselves under His mighty hand—and thus also in relation to everything that happens, especially the sufferings which they may have to endure for Christ's sake. Such an attitude and persistent activity of submission should be inspired by an awareness of God's sovereignty or providential control—i.e. all things are under His mighty hand—and by confidence in His loving care of His suffering people, and in His unfailing purpose for their present preservation and ultimate glorification. What Peter thus implies is, not only that God is in control of all that happens, but that, no matter what happens, He can be trusted to exercise His control for His people's good. Christians, therefore, should submit, not just to the circumstances, but in the circumstances to the hand that controls them (cf. Heb. xii. 7–9). In this awareness and confidence they should rightly refuse to be oppressed by anxiety or alarm, but rather should decisively throw them off upon the Lord.

Since the reference of the qualifying phrase *under the mighty hand of God* is to God's controlling providence, and particularly, in its familiar scriptural usage, to His ability to deliver His people, and to judge their enemies (see Ex. iii. 20, vii. 5; Dt. v. 15; 1 Ki. viii. 42), the imperative *Humble yourselves* virtually demands from believers in God not just passive resignation but active co-operation, i.e. 'allow yourselves to be humbled' (Selwyn). Compare, for example, the way in which a person in need of physical treatment and relief chooses and consents to become a patient of a particular surgeon, and thus submits himself under his 'operating hand', in the hope of enjoying the promised benefit in due time. The promise *that he may exalt you* recalls, and is explicitly grounded upon, the words of Christ Himself, e.g. Lk. xiv. 11. *In due time*, i.e., as Leighton puts it, 'not thy fancied time, but His own wisely appointed time'.

Verse 7 partly quotes and partly interprets the thought of
Ps. lv. 22, 'Cast thy burden upon the LORD, and he shall
sustain thee'. The quotation follows the LXX use of *merimna*,
'care', 'anxiety'. When troubles beset us we cannot just throw
them off, and thus abruptly get rid, or out of, them. But we
can and ought to get rid of the anxiety which they cause. We
can refuse to be burdened by care, which will get us down,
disturb our peace, distract our mind, because we can count on
the Lord's ability and readiness to help. *Merimna* comes from
a verbal root which means 'to divide'. Anxiety tends so to
distract and to divide the mind that it prevents wholehearted
devotion. The antidote for it is to turn to God and to find
relief in pouring out our anxiety upon Him. *Casting* translates
the verb *epiriptein*, 'to throw upon' (cf. Lk. xix. 35), a word
which suggests effort. Here the aorist tense of the participle
suggests a single decisive action. Such burdens ought to be
completely got rid of by a decisive act of committal and
surrender, in which they are cast upon God and cease to be
carried by us. As we thus confide in Him, He has promised to
sustain us, and to preserve us in peace of mind, i.e. free from
anxiety or alarm (see Is. xxvi. 3). *For he careth for you* expresses
a belief which is distinctive of Christianity and of biblical
faith. Other religions with their many ceremonies are commonly occupied with the business of making God care, 'of
awakening by sacrifice or prayer or act the slumbering interest
of the Deity' (Masterman). Christians begin with, and are
meant to build on, the confidence that God does care (cf. Mt.
vi. 25–35; Rom. v. 8, viii. 32).

8, 9. Such strong confidence in God as has just been expressed does not justify indulgence or carelessness. There is
still need to be thoroughly self-controlled and alert, which is
just what Peter himself failed to be when he denied Christ.
For we have an adversary who is always active and looking for
opportunity to overwhelm us. His aim is to sow discord, to
break fellowship, by malicious suggestion. He accuses God to
men, men to God, and men to each other. His aim is to

undermine confidence, to silence confession, to get us to stop believing. He ought to be resisted and opposed. We must stand our ground, strong in our Christian confidence. In this we should be helped and encouraged by realizing that we are not alone in this conflict nor are we having to face unusual hardship. Rather, such experience is the common lot of God's people as long as they are in this world. Participation in it is a mark of belonging to the brotherhood (cf. Heb. xii. 7, 8). Also such sufferings are no unfortunate mischance but part of the working out to its completion of God's purposes for His people's good. They will come to an end when those purposes are fulfilled.

Antidikos, your adversary, means an opponent in a lawsuit (cf. Lk. xii. 58, xviii. 3). *Diabolos, the devil*, i.e. a slanderer, or false accuser, is used in the LXX for the Hebrew 'Satan' (see Jb. i. 6–12; Zc. iii. 1). Both words suggest a malicious enemy who makes accusations and presses false charges (see Rev. xii. 9–11; cf. also 1 Pet. ii. 12, iii. 16, iv. 4).

Seeking whom he may devour; Whom resist stedfast in the faith. The danger in mind here is probably that of denying the faith, of being pressed or frightened into ceasing to confess Christ. This is the kind of pressure by which Peter was overcome when he denied his Lord. Jesus had spoken of such danger as imminent because of the activity of Satan. Also, Peter is obviously here seeking to do what the Lord told him to do after his own recovery from failure, namely, to strengthen his brethren (see Lk. xxii. 31, 32). In support of this interpretation note that in Rev. xii. 9–11 the devil is said to have been overcome by faithful testimony and fearless devotion unto death. Also, 'in the letter written by the churches of Lyons and Vienne during the persecution of Marcus Aurelius those who at first denied the faith and afterward repented and stood firm are described as being "devoured" by the beast and afterwards disgorged alive by him' (Blenkin). It is also noteworthy that while the other typical sources of danger to Christian believers—the world and the flesh—ought alike to be forsaken, and other interests pursued, the devil is an enemy who ought firmly to be resisted.

Your brethren translates *adelphotēs*, 'the brotherhood' or Christian community, here thought of as a distinct group and as a single unit in the world (cf. ii. 17). *Are* ('being', RV mg.) *accomplished.* The verb *epiteleisthai* (present continuous tense) suggests that the afflictions are being completed or perfected, that some intended purpose in them has yet to be finished.

XIII. CONCLUDING ASSURANCE AND PERSONAL GREETING (v. 10-14)

God Himself in the wealth of His grace, as the One who has called them to share eternally in His own glory, can be counted on according to His purpose to use their brief earthly sufferings to make them strong and steadfast. For verily His is the strength that prevails always.

Because of his confidence in him as a faithful member of the brotherhood, Peter has used Silvanus to write this letter. It is all too brief. Its purpose is to encourage them, particularly by giving them his apostolic testimony concerning the true character of the grace of God, which is thus to be enjoyed in the midst of sufferings by humble, dependent and faithful souls. Let them stand fast therein.

The chosen church of God in the worldly city whence he writes, and particularly Mark, who is to Peter as his own son, send greetings. Let them keep alive among themselves similar expression of affectionate greeting. May they all be given to enjoy the peace which belongs to those who are in Christ Jesus.

10. The verbs here are future not optative (see RV). They express a promise not a wish. Peter is not praying that God may, but making an affirmation that God will, in order to give his readers assurance. God can thus be counted on to complete their salvation (cf. i. 5, 6), both because He is the *God of all grace*, and because He has actually called them to share in His own glory. The phrase *of all grace*, or 'of every grace' (cf. iv. 10, 'the manifold grace of God'), implies that God's grace covers every need and is available for every member of the Christian brotherhood. Three important truths are asserted concerning the divine calling: it is *by Christ Jesus*, or 'in Christ' (RV); it is *unto his eternal glory*; it is to find its fulfilment *after that ye have suffered a while*. It is, therefore, a calling similar to Christ's own, through earthly suffering to heavenly glory (cf. i. 11). Also, thus to share first in the suffering is as much part of their calling as to share finally in the glory (see ii. 20, 21). The contrast is emphasized between the eternal and divine character of the glory and the brief duration of the suffering—'a little while' (RV). This indicates the worthwhile nature of the end for which the suffering is to be endured. The prospect of the glory beyond it should enable Christians to view suffering in true perspective (cf. i. 6; 2 Cor. iv. 17).

Note the RV rendering 'God . . . shall himself perfect, stablish, strengthen you'. There is emphasis here on the direct, personal character of God's ministry to His people. In expression of His grace, and in fulfilment of the purpose of their calling, He cares for their progress and perfection Himself (cf. 1 Thes. v. 23, RV). 'It is no merely fortuitous or instrumental helps that are promised, but God's own active intervention and personal presence' (Selwyn). For *perfect* the RV mg. has 'restore'. The root meaning of the verb *katartizein* is 'to make fit or complete', 'to qualify for one's task'. It is used of mending nets (see Mk. i. 19; cf. 2 Tim. iii. 17, RV; Lk. vi. 40). *Stablish* means to make steadfast, as they were exhorted to be in the previous verse (cf. 2 Thes. ii. 17, iii. 3). This is the kind of ministry that Peter himself was instructed by our Lord to exercise towards his brethren (see Lk. xxii. 32). Masterman suggests that the distinctive meaning of *strengthen* may be 'to equip for active service'. The sequence of thought would then be that God will first establish them firmly in their own personal faith or give them strength to stand firm; and then empower them for active service, or give them strength to go on. *Settle* is added in most MSS, though it is open to question whether its inclusion here is original to the text.

11. There is no verb in the Greek of this verse. It may be the language of prayer, i.e. so may it be. It is more probably the language of acknowledgment and ascription, as in iv. 11, and in the familiar ending of the Lord's prayer, i.e. His is the dominion for ever. To this statement the 'Amen' adds emphatic endorsement. Such an assertion affords the fullest ground for confidence and courage. The noun *kratos*, 'strength' or 'might', AV and RV *dominion*, is used only of God in the New Testament. It describes the ability to keep under control, to acquire and to retain the mastery. This power belongs to God now and for eternity.

12. Peter probably at this point took the pen himself and added the closing postscript with his own hand (cf. 2 Thes. iii. 17). This *Silvanus* is usually identified with Paul's chosen companion on his second missionary journey (Acts xv. 40), and his associate in the writing of the letters to the Thessalonians (see 1 Thes. i. 1; 2 Thes. i. 1; 2 Cor. i. 19). In Acts Luke calls him 'Silas'. Like Paul he was both a Jew and a Roman citizen (see Acts xvi. 19, 20, 25, 37). It is possible that Silvanus is the Latin and Silas the Greek form of his original Aramaic name. *Sch'l' iach*, meaning 'sent', is the name suggested.

While the phraseology *by Silvanus . . . I have written* could mean that Silvanus was the messenger who was to carry the letter (cf. Acts xv. 23, where the same man was a bearer of the letters written after the council of Jerusalem), and while this was probably true, Peter's use here of *I have written* rather than 'I have sent' seems to imply that Peter also used Silvanus as his scribe. This would well explain how ideas rightly regarded as Peter's in origin are expressed in such good Greek.

In the Greek the wording and order of *a faithful brother unto you* are 'to you the faithful brother'. The position of 'to you' and the use of the definite article suggest that Silvanus was well known to Peter's intended readers, and that Peter is referring to his faithful ministry among them. The sense of *as I suppose* is better expressed by RV, 'as I account him'. Peter is not venturing on an uncertain expression of opinion, but indicating his firmly established regard for Silvanus' character and work.

For *I have written briefly*, cf. Heb. xiii. 22. This means that the letter is short and necessarily condensed compared with all that Peter would like to have written, or with all that Silvanus may say when he arrives. *Exhorting, and testifying* indicates explicitly Peter's twofold object in writing, to confirm their faith and hope in God by his apostolic witness to God's saving grace, and to encourage them to stand firm in it. *This is the true grace of God* seems to refer to the apostle's fundamental message, to which it is his calling and concern to testify, i.e. the message of the gospel of Christ in whom saving grace is extended to the unworthy and to the humble (i. 10, v. 5), making them heirs of life (iii. 7), and qualifying them to endure suffering here, and to enjoy eternal glory hereafter (v. 10). For *wherein ye stand* the RV reading, which renders an imperative rather than an indicative in the Greek, is to be preferred, i.e. 'stand ye fast therein' (cf. i. 13). This then sums up the exhortation which complements Peter's testimony.

13. In the phrase *the church that is at Babylon* the noun for 'church' does not occur in the Greek, but only the feminine definite article with a noun understood. It would also be possible, therefore, to treat it as a personal reference to Peter's wife. The name 'Babylon' is used in Rev. xvii, xviii to refer to Rome, and it can be so understood here. Only at and since the Reformation have some preferred to treat the word literally as a reference either to Babylon in Mesopotamia or to a military station called Babylon in Egypt.[1] Since in the opening salutations Peter described his intended readers in Asia Minor as 'elect . . . sojourners of the Dispersion' (i. 1, RV), it seems appropriate here that he should describe the Christian congregation in Rome as sharing the same election (*elected together with you*), and sojourning in Babylon itself, the world-centre of organized godlessness. Such a reference significantly enforces Peter's testimony in the preceding verses that the

---

[1] For a fuller discussion see *Introduction*, pp. 64 ff.

whole Christian brotherhood in the world shares in the same afflictions (v. 9), and can in the midst of them be made to stand by the same true grace of God (v. 12).

Marcus my son is presumably the same Mark who is mentioned both in Acts (xii. 12, 25, xv. 36–39), and in Paul's Epistles (Col. iv. 10; 2 Tim. iv. 11; Phm. 24), and who wrote the second Gospel. Strong early tradition says that in producing his Gospel record he was directly dependent upon Peter. Peter's description of him as 'my son' may witness either to Christian indebtedness or simply to personal human intimacy of relationship. Since there is other evidence for Mark's presence in Rome, this helps to confirm the view that Peter also was in Rome when he wrote this Epistle. It is not possible, however, decisively to sort out the exact chronology of either Peter's residence in Rome or Mark's relations there both with Paul and with Peter.

14. Peter is concerned that Christians meeting locally should actively express towards each other the affection and goodwill he would wish similarly to express could he himself physically be present. An actual *kiss* seems to have been in common use when Christians met in fellowship and for worship as an outward sign of unity and love (cf. Rom. xvi. 16; 1 Cor. xvi. 20; 2 Cor. xiii. 12; 1 Thes. v. 26).

Peter ends with a simple, significant, comprehensive description of Christians, *all that are in Christ*. It indicates that participation in the blessing and fellowship of the gospel depends entirely upon direct personal relation to the Messiah. None can enjoy them apart from Him; all may enjoy them who belong to Him.

THE TEACHING OF THE EPISTLE

I. THE NATURE OF GOD

From the many references to God in 1 Peter, most of which are
the more significant because they are so incidental, we may
learn much concerning God's sovereignty, character and ways.

He is 'the God' (the Greek has the definite article, *ho Theos*;
i. 3, ii. 17), and 'God the Father' or 'the God and Father of
our Lord Jesus Christ' (i. 2, 3); that is, He is the one true God,
and the first Person of the Trinity. He may also be called on as
'Father' by His redeemed people (i. 17). Others must in the
end know Him as the Judge, who, when the time comes, will
judge all, living and dead (iv. 5). He will, too, judge 'according
to every man's work', and 'without respect of persons' (i. 17).
Nor should Christians forget that God's judgment is active
now, and must begin at His own house. This awareness should
make them spend their earthly lives both restrained by reverence and sustained in confidence (see i. 17, ii. 23, iv. 17–19).
For God regards the righteous and hears their prayers, but He
opposes evil-doers (iii. 12). He resists the proud and gives
grace to the humble (v. 5). His people, therefore, should acknowledge His mighty hand, submit to it, and expect vindication by it in due time (v. 6).

God is to be acknowledged and blessed (i. 3) as the author
of the salvation of His people. This salvation was determined
or foreordained by Him before the foundation of the world. Its
fulfilment is according to His foreknowledge (i. 2, 20). He it is
who has raised Christ up from the dead, and given Him glory.
This gives those who believe in Him solid ground for confidence and hope (see i. 3, 21).

God has for His people His own will. It is in obedience or
devotion to His will that their lives should henceforth be lived

(i. 2, iv. 2). In the freedom which He has made theirs in Christ, they are to face life as His servants (ii. 16). Their conduct should be of a kind which is acceptable with God, and in His sight of great price (ii. 20, iii. 4). So in all things ought He to be glorified (iv. 11), for His is the glory and the dominion for ever (v. 11).

He is a God of holiness (i. 15, 16), mercy (i. 3), grace (v. 10) and longsuffering (iii. 20). His word lives and abides (i. 23, 25). He is therefore rightly to be feared or reverenced (i. 17, ii. 17). Such awareness of God should make His people live differently, and in a way they would never otherwise do (ii. 19). This is the more true because God has openly shown that He can be trusted (i. 21). Because His people know that He cares for them, they may cast all their anxiety upon Him (v. 7). Towards them He manifests His grace in manifold ways; e.g. by giving them abilities for mutual service (iv. 10, 11).

Admittedly, it may be God's will for His people to suffer here on earth, even for well-doing (iii. 17, iv. 19). He uses such suffering to test and to mature their faith (i. 6, 7), and thus to make them perfect (v. 10). So those who suffer should commit themselves to His faithfulness as the Creator (iv. 19), even as the Christ Himself, when suffering unjustly at men's hands, 'committed himself to him that judgeth righteously' (ii. 23).

II. THE PERSON AND WORK OF JESUS CHRIST

In this Epistle it is implied at once that Jesus Christ, whose apostle the writer claims to be (i. 1), is both the Son of God and the Lord of the Church or the elect community. For the one eternal God is said to be His 'Father', and He is described as 'our Lord' (i. 3). God determined for Him in eternity a purpose to be fulfilled in history; He was foreordained before the foundation of the world to redeem His people by His sacrifice unto blood, i.e. by His death on earth as man (i. 18–20). In Old Testament times, before His personal appearing on earth, the Spirit, whose work it is to speak of Him, bore witness through the testimony of prophets to the sufferings which were destined to befall Him as Messiah, and to the glories which, as a consequence, would assuredly be His (i. 10, 11).

This eternal divine purpose has now found fulfilment. As a veritable consummation of earthly history Christ has been manifested here on earth, as was foreordained (i. 20). He has suffered in the flesh as man (iv. 1). He was 'put to death in the flesh' (iii. 18). As one still active in the spirit beyond death He went and preached to the imprisoned evil spirits, heralding His own triumph, now fully sure, once His earthly sacrifice was complete (iii. 19). God set His seal upon this, and gave to sinful men, otherwise without hope, a new ground of confidence by raising Jesus from the dead and giving Him glory (i. 3, 21). Jesus was thus divinely exalted; He went into heaven and was enthroned at God's right hand as Lord over all heavenly powers and authorities (iii. 22). This same Jesus is yet to be unveiled and thus openly manifested (i. 7); His destined glory is to be fully revealed (iv. 13). Peter thus speaks in confident testimony because he has himself been an eye-witness of Christ's sufferings, and because, on the mount of our Lord's transfiguration, he was also given a pre-view of Christ's heavenly glory, which is yet to be revealed (v. 1).

The work that Christ thus did through incarnation and earthly suffering results not only in heavenly glories for Him, but also in both present and eternal benefits for those for whom He suffered. For at His unveiling, whether one thinks of His first advent or of His final manifestation, grace is brought to His people (i. 13).

His earthly work was brought to a head in His death, that is by His blood-shedding on the cross. There He was offered, like a flawless and spotless lamb, to procure redemption for those in bondage (i. 18, 19). He fulfilled what was anticipated typically in Old Testament times by the redemption of the Israelites from bondage and judgment in Egypt at the time when the passover lambs were slain and their blood sprinkled on the door posts.

The death that Christ died was the kind of death due to wrong-doers. He was publicly executed, exposed to the shame and curse of hanging on a tree, as one bearing the extreme penalty of sin. He suffered as a proxy or substitute, the righteous One in the place of the unrighteous many. This He did to bring to them healing, renewal and reconciliation, and thus to bring them to God (ii. 24, iii. 18). For, since His blood has once for all been shed, it is, metaphorically speaking, henceforth continually available to be sprinkled on the sin-stained and the outsider, to assure them of cleansing and acceptance in God's sight and of participation in the blessings of the new covenant of grace eternally sealed by His death (i. 2).

Though Christ risen, exalted and enthroned is not now to be seen, as He once was and yet will be, communion with Him is enjoyed by His people through the response of personal love, faith and committal (i. 8). He is to be sanctified as Lord in their hearts (iii. 15, RV). He grants to them by the Spirit His indwelling presence, thus making their hearts His earthly temple (iv. 14). Not only so, they are also called together to realize a corporate relation to Him as a new, divinely-integrated fellowship. For He is by divine appointment the living stone, divinely chosen and honoured, and set in place by God in the heavenly Zion, to be the chief corner stone of a building, whose component stones are living people. For all who come to Him, and taste His grace, are intended to be built into a temple, or to belong to a priesthood whose privilege it is to offer to God spiritual sacrifices. These are acceptable to God, because of their personal relation to Christ, and their continuing confidence in His mediation. He is thus the spiritual Shepherd or Bishop of a new flock which is constituted as wandering sinners repent and return to God through Him (ii. 3-5, 25).

In the accomplishment of His earthly career Christ also left His people an example to be followed, and gave them an indication or norm of the character and course of their new Christian calling. For He was sinless both in deed and word; He 'did no sin, neither was guile found in his mouth'. Under the pain and provocation of unjust treatment He did not revile

His persecutors, but in silence committed His cause to God, counting on the sure outworking of God's righteous and faithful dealing (ii. 20–23, iv. 19).

Also, our Lord's own course as the Christ makes plain that two features are essential and complementary in its completion. One is earthly suffering now, and the other heavenly glory hereafter. So Christ's people should count participation in both as essential parts of their Christian calling and privilege. They are to rejoice inasmuch as they are partakers of Christ's sufferings now so that, when His glory shall be revealed, they may be glad also with exceeding joy (i. 11, iv. 13, v. 10).

Finally, there is a solemn other side to these purposes of God for His Christ. For in His earthly appearing as the promised Messiah the very eternal Son of God is his suffering to sorrow. The very stone, which God exalted to be the head of the corner, was rejected by the earthly ecclesiastical builders. It was part of the earthly lot of the Christ, who did God's will and fulfilled God's eternal purpose, to be rejected by men, to be rejected even by religious leaders who professed to be doing God service. To them the chosen stone of God became 'a stone of stumbling, and a rock of offence'. Thus the events of Christ's earthly life and the prophetic comment of the inspired Scripture alike make plain that the same Jesus, who is appointed of God to be a source of endless blessings to those who believe, becomes, because of their own rebellious self-will, an inevitable cause of judgment and undoing to the disobedient (ii. 3, 7, 8).

III. THE WORK OF THE HOLY SPIRIT

This Epistle also contains a few noteworthy references to the activity of the Spirit of God, and to His co-operation in the accomplishment of the fore-ordained purposes of God the Father for His Son, and, through Him, for His elect and redeemed people. Before the Son's manifestation on earth the Spirit, in direct association with the Son's Person and work as the Messiah or Christ, testified beforehand through prophets of the sufferings and glories destined for the Christ, and of the saving grace of God that would thus come to men, particularly to Gentile outsiders. We may, therefore, so Peter implies, still rightly look to the Old Testament Scriptures for Spirit-inspired witness to these Christian and evangelical truths (see i. 10–12).

After Christ's earthly work was finished the Holy Spirit was specially sent from heaven to empower for evangelization, and to ensure that the truths prophetically revealed in the Scriptures should now, in the day of their fulfilment, be preached to those whom they are destined to benefit (see i. 12. Cf. Lk. xxiv. 44–49; Acts i. 8).

The same Spirit is active as the Sanctifier. He brings the elect into the actual enjoyment of the blessings made available for them in Christ, through His shed blood, and according to the promises of God's covenant thus ratified. It is the Spirit's work to produce obedience in God's people, i.e. the outworking of holiness in character and conduct (see i. 2).

The Spirit also specially comes to rest upon God's people in this world,—as did the pillar of cloud or fire on the tabernacle in the wilderness, symbolizing the divine presence (see Ex. xxxiii. 9, 10, xl. 34–38),—so that they become sensible of God's presence with them, particularly when they suffer reproach for the name of Christ. See iv. 14.

It is also noteworthy that this Epistle refers to the distinct and combined presence and activity of all three Persons of the Trinity, the Father, the Son, and the Holy Spirit, explicitly in i. 2, and possibly in iv. 14.

IV. THE PEOPLE OF GOD

a. Their divine election, redemption, sanctification

Peter addresses his readers as people given a new status and experience by the eternal determination and the earthly intervention of the living God. They are 'elect according to the foreknowledge of God the Father' (i. 2). They are redeemed not with corruptible things, 'but with the precious blood of Christ' (i. 18, 19). Grace has been brought unto them by His

appearing (i. 10–13). The eternal Son of God, whom God predestined, before the world was created, to do this work, has been
manifested in history for their sake to accomplish this work of
redemption (i. 20). By God's resurrection of Christ from the
dead, and His exaltation of Him to heavenly glory, they have
been divinely assured that they can now, through Christ, look
to God in faith and hope (i. 3, 21). The word of God, His gospel of saving grace, has been preached unto them in the con-
victing power of the Spirit (i. 12, 25). Their response to this
truth—a response expressed in baptism (iii. 21, 22)—has been
followed by the promised benefits of cleansing and quickening.
They are 'purified' and 'born again' (i. 22, 23). The Spirit has
become their active sanctifier (i. 2). They who 'in time past
were not a people, . . . are now the people of God' (ii. 10). 'The
God of all grace', who has called them by Christ Jesus not only
into present death to sins and life to righteousness (ii. 24) but
also 'unto his eternal glory', can be trusted, after they have
suffered a while, to make them perfect, to stablish, strengthen
and settle them (v. 10).

b. *Their heavenly calling*

The elect people of God are called by Him to share in the fulfilment of purposes, whose consummation is not to be realized
on earth during their present lifetime, but in heaven and in the
coming day of God. God has called them into His eternal
glory (v. 10). They are destined to possess 'an inheritance incorruptible, and undefiled, and that fadeth not away, reserved
in heaven' for them (i. 4). They are intended to enjoy a salvation, which is prepared for open manifestation in the fulness of
God's time (i. 5). Therefore they may count on being preserved by God's power until the day of full possession, provided
that they believe and keep on believing in Him (i. 5). Having
tasted, through His coming to redeem, how gracious the Lord
is (ii. 3), they should go on hoping to the end for the grace that
is to be brought to them at the final revelation of Jesus Christ
(i. 13). This prospect should cause them at all times greatly to
rejoice (i. 6, 8). They should also live in the light of this im-

pending consummation, as those aware that 'the end of all things is at hand' (iv. 7). They should anticipate the day when Christ's glory will be revealed, and desire so to live now as to share the more in exceeding joy then (iv. 13). For faithful service now will be rewarded then with 'a crown of glory that fadeth not away' (v. 4). When Christ is unveiled, present faith in God, faith which is very precious in His sight and whose genuineness present trials are intended to put to the test, will shine forth and bring praise and honour and glory to Him (i. 7).

c. Their distinctive Christian behaviour

Some things which have been written already have indicated that those who become God's people in Christ must disclose their new relationship and status by radical changes of conduct. It seems worth while, however, to survey the chief features of such distinctive Christian behaviour separately. Let us notice four of them.

i. Coming to Christ. The decisive initial human response to the Christian gospel is for men individually to come to Christ, and to believe in Him (ii. 4-7). For God has set Christ in the heavenly Zion as the chief corner-stone, and has promised satisfying benefit to every individual who comes to confide in Him. In this way all who become Christians taste, each for himself or herself, that the Lord is gracious. Or again, God calls men out of darkness into His marvellous light (ii. 9). This makes those who were going astray like sheep to come back to acknowledge Christ as the Shepherd and Bishop of their souls (ii. 25). They become obedient to the truth and find God-given cleansing and quickening (i. 22, 23). In their baptism, which is the visible seal of such purification and regeneration, they are assured of the personal enjoyment of salvation, not because the ceremonial use of water has any power to remove moral defilement or create a new nature, but through the sincerity, when questioned, of their own answering confession of faith in Christ crucified, risen and exalted (iii. 18-22).

ii. Ceasing from sin and becoming holy. Such repentance from sin and faith towards Christ make a corresponding twofold moral demand, a demand to which actual personal response is made possible by Christ's death and resurrection. For Christ bore men's sins in His body on the tree in order that their connection with sins might be terminated, and in order that they might begin to live a new life of righteousness (ii. 24). Christians are consequently challenged to arm themselves with the same mind (iv. 1), and to recognize that the purpose of Christ's death and resurrection is to secure that all who acknowledge Him as their sin-bearer and Lord may cease from spending their time in sinful self-indulgence, and may devote the rest of their earthly lives to the doing of God's will (iv. 2). The very price and purpose of redemption from sin (i. 18, 19) and the new relation to God as Father into which Christians are thus brought (i. 14–17) combine to place upon them the inescapable obligation henceforth to live worthily, to reproduce the likeness of the family to which they belong, to become holy, as God Himself is holy, in every aspect of their behaviour. Because they are begotten of God (i. 23), all wickedness of thought and spirit, of word and deed, can and ought to be put away (ii. 1). They must cease to gratify harmful carnal appetites (ii. 11). They must turn away from evil, and do good (iii. 11). This is the only proper outworking of genuine obedience to the truth.

iii. Persistently doing good. The active practice of right living must not only be begun, but also continued. Christians should love one another as brethren in Christ with genuine and fervent love (i. 22), and with a practical readiness to render one another humble service (v. 5). In a spirit of willing, submissive co-operation, and recognizing that such human relations are in principle divinely ordained, they should accept, and faithfully discharge, their responsibilities in civil, community and family life (ii. 13–iii. 7). For it is now God's will for them that by such well-doing they should silence slanderous misrepresentation and win some, otherwise unresponsive, to faith in Christ.

Thus to do good, to seek peace and to pursue it (iii. 10–12) is the positive way of life and of true blessedness. Christians should, therefore, persist in well-doing no matter what treatment they receive in return (iv. 19). They should not render 'evil for evil, or railing for railing: but contrariwise (be) blessing' (iii. 9). For, says Peter, 'hereunto were ye called, that ye should inherit a blessing' (RV). Such steadfastness will be possible only if they show mental alertness and disciplined sobriety (i. 13, iv. 7), and if, in defiance of the devil, and in dependence upon God, they watch and pray (v. 6–9).

iv. Patiently enduring evil,—particularly the evil of unjust suffering. In such a world as this such suffering is inevitable both for conscience' sake, and for Christ's sake (ii. 19, iv. 13–16). When called to face it they should remember Christ's example, and follow His steps (ii. 21), rejoicing at the privilege of sharing His reproach, and anticipating the prospect of sharing His glory.

d. Their corporate fellowship

Although the actual Greek word *ecclēsia*, i.e. 'church', does not occur in this Epistle, Christians are here explicitly instructed to think of themselves as members of the divine community. Though they sojourn in this world scattered in many different places, they share a common election and a common Lord (i. 1–3); and so they constitute in the world a distinct and single 'brotherhood' (v. 9; the Greek word *adelphotēs* is in the singular with the definite article; see RV mg.), whose members all share in the same accomplishment of inevitable and divinely-foreordained sufferings.

All who come to Christ are intended of God to come to Him as 'a chief corner stone', and by direct personal relation to Him themselves to find their place 'as living stones' in a building or spiritual house, in which God dwells and is worshipped (ii. 4–6). Christians, therefore, may be simply described as 'all that are in Christ' (v. 14). Not only so, because these 'stones' are 'living' people, they are intended to constitute, not only the temple or shrine, but also the separated priesthood to offer through Christ spiritual sacrifices well-pleasing to God. Again it is their direct personal relation to Christ that makes such ministry both possible and acceptable.

Christians are also to regard themselves as belonging to, as together called to constitute, 'an elect race, a royal priesthood, a holy nation, a people for God's own possession' (ii. 9, RV). This means that those who formerly had no corporate unity are now not only a people, but God's own people (ii. 10); and they are intended to offer God worship and to cause God's virtues or 'excellencies' to be made known (ii. 9, RV) by what they are, and by what they do, together as one people.

It is of urgent practical importance, therefore, that Christians should recognize one another as brethren in Christ, and actively practise fellowship. Four times Peter exhorts them to love one another, because they are now brethren (i. 22, ii. 17, iii. 8, iv. 8). This duty is forced upon them as an immediate consequence of obeying the truth; indeed, it should be a genuine unaffected expression of pure and sustained, God-given, heart love for one another. Sympathy, tenderheartedness, humble-mindedness, hospitality, and active ministry should all be deliberately practised towards fellow-Christians (iii. 8, iv. 8–11). They must recognize that the gifts, which God has given to them individually, are meant to be exercised in the service of one another.

Christians ought also to think of themselves as God's flock (v. 2). For, as those who were like wandering sheep going astray, they have found needed care, guidance and provision by returning to acknowledge Christ as the Shepherd and Bishop of their souls (ii. 25). It is this new common personal relation to Him that makes them one; and this means that there is only one flock of God; for there is only one chief Shepherd. Care of the sheep in this flock is allotted locally to elders (v. 1–4), who function as under-shepherds or as bishops, exercising oversight (v. 2, Greek *episkopein*). They are to do their work, not by lording it over the sheep, but by making themselves ensamples to them, that is, by leading not driving.

V. THE PLACE OF SUFFERING

Great prominence is given in this Epistle to the place in God's purpose of the sufferings both of Christ and of His people. Far from being offended by the idea that God's Christ should suffer, or thinking it strange that God's people should suffer, Christians are here challenged to welcome suffering as essential both to present earthly progress and to final heavenly fulfilment. Let us notice in detail the main aspects of Peter's treatment of this theme.

a. Suffering in this world was foreordained for God's Christ

The prophets of Old Testament times, who were moved by the Spirit to anticipate the crowning manifestation of God's saving grace towards sinful men, testified beforehand concerning the sufferings which must happen to the Messiah (i. 10, 11). Sufferings are here implicitly treated as something which must inevitably be faced if God is to intervene in the world to save men. For, in the scriptural revelation of God's purpose, to become Messiah and to endure suffering belong together. The eternal Son of God could not become the one without setting His face to endure the other.

b. Suffering is an inevitable experience of the doer of righteousness in a sinful world

No-one can set himself to live a godly life, as Paul puts it (2 Tim. iii. 12), without the possibility of having to face persecution. Virtuous and conscientious behaviour may involve a man in wrongful suffering (ii. 19). This is supremely illustrated in the earthly course of Christ Himself (ii. 21–23). For He was sinless in deed and word. Yet He was reviled, and made to suffer. So others can expect no exemption from similar treatment. Rather they should remember that 'this is thankworthy', or pleasing to God, and 'acceptable' (RV) with Him, 'if a man for conscience toward God endure grief, suffering wrongfully'. So any who suffer for righteousness' sake are to be reckoned happy or blessed (iii. 14).

c. Suffering, particularly the extreme suffering of the death penalty by Christ for sinners, is the consequence and the only cure of sin

Such suffering had to be borne by the righteous for the unrighteous, by Christ as the Redeemer and Reconciler of sinners (iii. 18). He bare our sins by suffering in His human body the extreme penalty of public execution on a cross (ii. 24). This sets us free from the entail of our sins. By the stripes which He bore, we are healed. Because He has thus died for our sins, He can bring us to God. By entering in mind into an awareness that Christ thus suffered in the flesh for our sins, we can and ought to cease from sinning and self-indulgence and henceforth live to do God's will (iv. 1, 2).

d. Suffering is in this world a distinctive part and privilege of the Christian's calling

It should therefore be endured patiently (ii. 20, 21). All who belong to Christ and would be publicly associated with Him in this world are liable to have to suffer on that account. They should count themselves happy when allowed to share in suffering for Christ's sake and as His people (iii. 14, 17, iv. 12–16), remembering that such afflictions are the common lot of the Christian brotherhood throughout the world (v. 9). God can and does use such suffering for His own predetermined ends, to test faith (i. 6, 7), to mature character (v. 10), to purge conduct (iv. 16, 17), and to bring praise and glory to Christ through the manifestation in His suffering people of His grace and patience, His peace and joy (i. 7). So Christians should know that their sufferings are no strange mistake (iv. 12), but according to God's will (iv. 19). In quiet confidence they should persist in well-doing, refraining from all retaliation and committing themselves and their cause, as Christ Himself did, to God the faithful Creator and the righteous Judge (ii. 23, iv. 19).

e. Suffering was for Christ, and is for His people, the way to glory

The prophets who foresaw the sufferings which must happen to the Messiah, foresaw also 'the glories that should follow them' (i. 10, 11, RV). Peter speaks in this letter not only as 'a witness of the sufferings of Christ', but also as 'a partaker of the glory that shall be revealed' (v. 1). After Christ had suffered, 'being put to death in the flesh', He was raised and exalted to the right hand of God, 'angels and authorities and powers being made subject unto him' (iii. 18, 21, 22). Since God thus gave Christ glory, our faith and hope may confidently be placed in God (i. 21).

Similarly it is those who are partakers of Christ's sufferings here, who, when His glory shall be revealed, will be glad with exceeding joy (iv. 13). For the God of all grace has called us into His eternal glory in Christ (v. 10). But He will bring us to this goal only after we have suffered a little while. For God will use the sufferings to perfect, stablish, strengthen us.

VI. THE INEVITABILITY OF GOD'S JUDGMENT

Because God judges righteously (ii. 23), because He without respect of persons judges according to each man's work (i. 17), sin wherever and in whomsoever it is found must be dealt with by God in judgment. To Him the living and dead must all give account (iv. 5). This is a terrifying prospect. Well may Peter ask, 'where shall the ungodly and the sinner appear?' (iv. 18). There is, however, a divinely-provided way of escape, a way of salvation and sanctification for sinners, through the inevitable judgment of God being accomplished here in the flesh, or in the body, first, in the decisive once-for-all sin-bearing by Christ on the tree (ii. 24, iii. 18) and, second, in the remedial chastisement and purging of providential divine discipline (iv. 16-19). 'For the time is come that judgment must begin at the house of God.' Judgment is thus wrought out here 'according to men in the flesh' (iv. 6), that God's people, thus reconciled to Him and purged from defilement, may live eternally hereafter 'according to God in the spirit'. Such an experience makes them like those in the ark at the time of the flood who did not escape judgment, but passed safely through it to emerge into a new world no longer undergoing judgment

(iii. 20, 21). It is to such a salvation, through the judgment that fell upon Christ in His death, that baptism into Christ bears witness. What such teaching also makes plain is that Christ is not continuing His atoning work in heaven, nor is there a purgatory for the people of God after death. Rather, all judgment is in Christ consummated for His people here and at death, that there may be life 'unto righteousness' and life 'according to God in the spirit' hereafter (ii. 24, iv. 6).

VII. THE FINAL OPEN MANIFESTATION OF CHRIST'S GLORY

Finally, it is in place, even at the cost of some repetition, to emphasize that the dominant note of this Epistle is one of confidence and hope (i, 3, 21), God's people have set before them the sure prospect of the full vindication and open glorification of the Christ whom they know as their Shepherd. He who has already been raised from the dead, exalted to God's right hand, and given glory (i. 21, iii. 22) is to be openly revealed and made manifest (i. 7, 13, v. 4). His glory will then be completely realized and fully displayed (iv. 13). Of this revelation of His glory Peter had a preview on the mount of our Lord's transfiguration (v. 1; cf. 2 Pet. i. 16–18). Those also who know, love and trust Him now, as the unseen Lord, have a foretaste of the unspeakable exceeding joy that will be fully experienced only when His glory is finally revealed openly (i. 8, iv. 13). It is when the chief Shepherd is thus manifested for all to see that the steadfast faith in Him of His people under earthly trial will openly bring to Him praise and honour and glory (i. 6, 7); and those who have been faithful in His service will themselves receive their own crown of glory (v. 4). This prospect should inspire His people to endure earthly trial with joy, as partakers of Christ's sufferings, that their joy, and indeed their personal share with Christ in His glory, may thus be all the greater in the day when His glory is revealed (iv. 12, 13; cf. Rom. viii. 18–20). 'Whose is the glory and the dominion for ever and ever' (iv. 11, RV).